Wideness

and Wonder

THE LIFE AND ART OF GEORGIA O'KEEFFE

BY SUSAN GOLDMAN RUBIN

chronicle books · san francisco

For my cousin Carol Coggan Barkoff —S. G. R.

First I wish to thank Agapita Judy Lopez, Rights and Reproductions Manager for Abiquiu Historic Properties, for her cooperation and guidance. I also want to thank Eumie Imm-Stroukoff, Librarian and Assistant Director of the Research Center Georgia O'Keeffe Museum; Paul Camp, Office Manager for Research UCLA Library; and Janet Hicks at ARS. Many thanks to my cousins Carol and Joel Barkoff for their hospitality in Albuquerque, and to my cousin Steve Berlin who provided maps to help me find the way to Santa Fe. I am enormously grateful to my editor Victoria Rock, associate editor Melissa Manlove, designer Natalie Davis, and to my entire publishing team at Chronicle for the time and care devoted to this book. I want to express particular appreciation to George Nicholson, agent, friend, and mentor, and to his assistant, Erica Silverman. Warmest thanks go to my Lunch Bunch friends for listening and critiquing. Most of all I thank my husband, Michael, especially for making a detour to York Beach, Maine.

Library of Congress Cataloging-in-Publication Data
Rubin, Susan Goldman.
Wideness and wonder : the life and art of Georgia O'Keeffe / by Susan Goldman Rubin.
p. cm.
Includes bibliographical references.
ISBN 978-0-8118-6983-6
1. O'Keeffe, Georgia, 1887–1986—Juvenile literature. 2. Painters—United States—Biography—Juvenile literature. I. O'Keeffe, Georgia, 1887–1986. II. Title. III. Title: Life and art of Georgia O'Keeffe.
ND237.O5R83 2010
759.13—dc22
2010008256

Book design by Natalie Davis.
Typeset in Neutra Text Book.

Manufactured in China

MIX
Paper from responsible sources
FSC® C104723
www.fsc.org

10 9 8 7 6 5 4 3 2

Chronicle Books LLC
680 Second Street, San Francisco, California 94107
www.chroniclekids.com

Contents

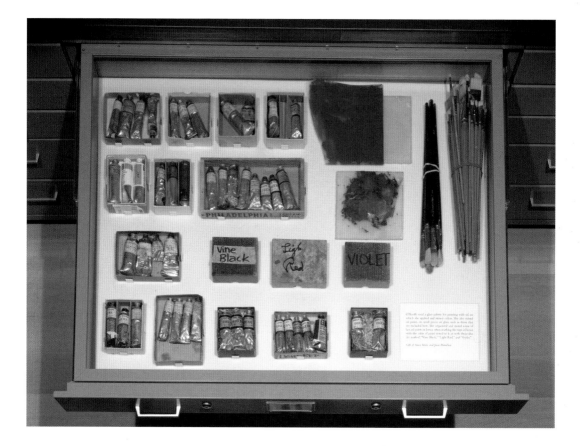

Display drawer at the Georgia O'Keeffe Research Center Library, showing pigments and brushes.

Author's note

When I began researching this book, I went to the Georgia O'Keeffe Museum in Santa Fe, New Mexico. At the Research Center, I peered through glass cases to examine her leather paint box, chunks of pastels, tubes of paint, brushes, and a glass palette. I opened drawers containing shells and animal bones she had saved, and even the navy blue sneakers she had worn.

The next day I drove to Abiquiu to visit her house. I was given a private tour by Judy Lopez, who had worked with Miss O'Keeffe toward the end of her life. As I roamed from room to room, and glimpsed the view of the highway from Miss O'Keeffe's bedroom, her collection of rocks on a window ledge, and her beloved door in the wall of the patio, I felt as though I were stepping into her paintings. Later I rode up to Ghost Ranch, Miss O'Keeffe's summer house. Beyond the house were the red hills dotted with sage and cottonwood trees that had inspired her, along with the flat-topped Cerro Pedernal, her "private mountain," which she included in so many paintings.

As I stood there blown by gusts of wind, I imagined what it was like for her living in the high desert, taking long walks, and collecting bleached animal bones to study and paint. Georgia O'Keeffe had said, "I have used these things to say what is to me the wideness and wonder of the world."

Georgia O'Keeffe, 1903, age sixteen.

I am going to be an artist

Georgia O'Keeffe's first visual memory was of the patchwork quilt she used to sit on when she was eight or nine months old. She vividly remembered the two patterns: white with small red stars, and black with a red and white flower.

Georgia, the second oldest of seven children, was born on November 15, 1887, in Sun Prairie, Wisconsin. Her father, Francis "Frank" O'Keeffe, was a farmer. Her mother, Ida Totto, was a well-educated woman who had hoped to become a doctor, but her schooling was cut short when she married. However, she always maintained her interest in education.

Ida loved books and spent hours reading aloud to her children. "It was particularly for my older brother [Francis], whose eyes were not good," recalled Georgia. So the books were mainly boys' stories of the Wild West. Tales of Kit Carson and Billy the Kid thrilled Georgia, and she dreamed of someday going to Texas.

Although she adored her mother's storytelling, Georgia felt closer to her father. She shared his love of the land. Growing up on a farm gave her a sensitivity to nature that would be a lasting influence on her art. Eventually, Georgia came to realize that Francis was her mother's favorite, and she and her brother grew apart. "I didn't mind at all," said Georgia in an interview.

"It left me very free." Since she felt too grown-up to play with her baby sisters, Georgia spent more and more time by herself. And she began to draw.

"The first thing I can remember drawing was a picture of a man lying on his back with his feet up in the air," she wrote in her autobiography. Georgia had drawn the figure on a paper bag. When she turned it around to make it look as though the figure was standing and bending over the drawing gave her a feeling of "real achievement."

Even when Georgia started school just before her fifth birthday, she didn't mingle much with other children. Georgia went to the one-room Town Hall School that her parents had also attended. Although the other first graders were a year older, Georgia kept up because she was bright and curious. "She would suddenly ask the most precise, unexpected questions," remembered her teacher.

When Georgia was eleven, her mother arranged for her and her younger sisters Ida and Anita to have drawing lessons from the Town Hall School teacher who boarded with them. They copied geometric shapes—cubes, cylinders, and spheres—from a drawing manual in a series by Louis Prang, which was popular at the time. No one considered Georgia particularly talented. Her sister Ida seemed to be the gifted one.

When Georgia was twelve, she and her sisters went into town every Saturday afternoon to study art. Their teacher told them to each choose a picture from a stack of reproductions of paintings she kept in her cupboard, and to copy it. For the first time, Georgia painted with watercolor, a medium that was to become one of her favorites.

At home Georgia copied a picture of a lighthouse from a geography book. The picture looked empty, so she added a horizon line and some palm trees, then a sun. She darkened the sun too much, so in her second lighthouse painting she made a cloudy sky.

One day when Georgia was in the eighth grade, she was at school with her friend Lena, daughter of the O'Keeffes' laundress. She asked Lena what she was going to do when she grew up. Lena said she didn't know. Georgia surprised herself by blurting, "I am going to be an artist." At that moment, Georgia didn't have a clear idea of what an artist was. But her mind was made up.

Untitled (Catherine O'Keeffe), 1904.

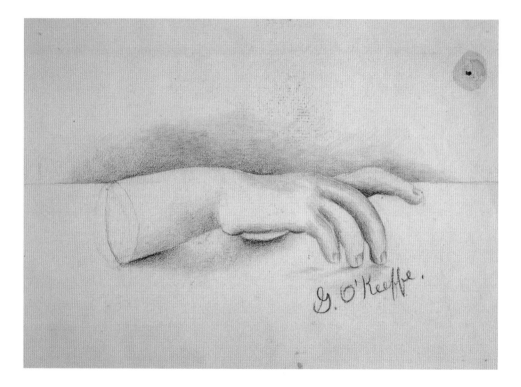

Untitled (Hand), 1902.

All kinds of Mischief 2

In the fall of 1901, when Georgia was almost fourteen, she entered the Sacred Heart Convent School in Madison, Wisconsin. The convent school, run by Dominican nuns, had strict rules. Visitors could come only on Saturday afternoons. The nuns inspected the students' books and read their personal mail. But Georgia didn't mind. "I don't even remember wanting to do anything I shouldn't," she said. On Sundays the girls were required to dress entirely in black. Georgia liked the style so much that for the rest of her life she wore plain clothes, usually black.

During her first art class there, Georgia and the other students were given some charcoal. The teacher, Sister Angelique, put a white plaster cast of a baby's hand on the table and told the girls to draw it. Georgia worked hard at her drawing. But Sister Angelique criticized Georgia in front of the whole class. "I was so embarrassed that it was difficult not to cry." The Sister drew some lines on Georgia's paper to show her what she thought was the right way to go about it. Georgia said, "It looked very strange to me—not at all beautiful like my own drawing." However, she wanted to please her teacher, and so she made larger drawings with lighter lines. At the end of the year, Sister Angelique exhibited Georgia's work and awarded her a gold pin "for improvement in illustration and drawing." Georgia also won a gold medal for good behavior.

The next year, she and Francis attended a public high school in Madison and lived with their aunt Lola. Georgia's most memorable experience at high school happened in the art room. She didn't think much of the art teacher, a thin woman who "wore her hat in school—a hat made all of artificial violets." Yet Georgia watched transfixed as the teacher stood in front of the class and held up a plant called a jack-in-the-pulpit. She pointed out the "strange shapes and variations in color, from the deep, almost black earthy violet through all the greens," said Georgia. Although Georgia had seen many jacks before on her family's farm, this was the first time she had thought of closely examining the flower. "I was a little annoyed at being interested because I didn't like the teacher," she wrote. "But maybe she started me looking at things—looking very carefully at details."

The visual memory stayed with Georgia, and years later she was to paint a bold series of oils depicting close-up views of a jack-in-the-pulpit.

That winter the weather was brutally cold. Her father, at home on the farm, was afraid of coming down with tuberculosis. His three brothers had died of the disease, and he thought he might stay healthier in a milder climate. So in March 1903, Georgia's parents sold their farm and bought a house and land in Williamsburg, Virginia.

In the fall, just before her sixteenth birthday, Georgia entered Chatham Episcopal Institute, a girls' school. As young Southern ladies, Georgia and her classmates were preparing for futures as well-mannered wives. Strict rules were enforced. The girls had to be in bed by ten o'clock with lights out. Georgia and her classmates were only permitted to take an afternoon walk in a line headed by a teacher. This time Georgia rebelled. She said, "I used to stand there and think, 'Now what can I do that I shouldn't do and not get caught?'"

Her classmates enjoyed her lively, mischievous ways. She got out of bed after the 10 p.m. bell rang. She fried biscuits on the little wooden stove in her

Untitled (Vase of Flowers), 1903/1905.

bedroom. She even taught the girls how to play poker, a forbidden game that she had learned from the farmhands in Sun Prairie. The few times Georgia got caught for breaking the rules, she was punished by having to spend Saturday copying some trite sayings over and over.

From the moment she arrived at Chatham, Georgia attracted attention. The other girls wore tight-fitting dresses with ruffles, but Georgia wore a plain, loose suit. Most of the girls had elaborate hairdos and oversized bows. In contrast, "Georgia's hair was drawn smoothly back from her broad, prominent forehead and she had no bow on her head at all, only one at the bottom of her pigtail," recalled a classmate.

During her two years at Chatham, Georgia studied art with Elizabeth Mae Willis, who was also the principal. Mrs. Willis recognized Georgia's talent and gave her her own table in the studio and permission to work there in the evenings by herself. Georgia's easel stood in the center of the room. "Here [Georgia] would stand for hours, perfectly silent, working on something that seemed to us already finished, adding colors that our ordinary eyes could never see," said a classmate.

Georgia painted many studies of flowers and gave them as gifts. However, she remembered only two things she painted at Chatham: "a large bunch of purple lilacs and some red and yellow corn." She said, "I remember wondering how I could paint the big shapes of bunches of lilacs—and at the same time—each little flower."

On graduation day, June 5, 1905, the girls talked eagerly about going home and getting ready for "dreamy dancing and cotillions." Not Georgia. She announced, "I am going to live a different life from the rest of you girls. I am going to give up everything for my art."

The class of 1905, Chatham Hall. Georgia is third from the right.

Untitled (Teapot and Flowers), 1903/1905.

Drawing from life 3

After graduation Georgia realized that she needed formal training to become an artist. So at age seventeen she set out to study at the School of the Art Institute of Chicago, one of the best fine arts colleges in America. In those early days of the twentieth century, it was considered daring for a young woman to be an art student. However, Georgia's mother approved completely, and Mrs. Willis, her former teacher at Chatham, encouraged her to develop her talent.

Later Georgia admitted that as she rode the train away from home, she felt "a very special sort of sick feeling." Nevertheless, she was determined to achieve her goal. She had considered going to the famed Art Students League in New York City, but her parents preferred the Midwest, where she could live with her mother's brother and sister, Uncle Charles and Aunt Ollie. Their apartment was within walking distance of the Art Institute.

Courses there were strictly based on the traditional programs offered in European art schools. Georgia began her studies with a basic drawing class. She and forty-three other students set up their easels in one of the museum's main galleries and were told to draw a white plaster cast of a male torso. "It didn't particularly interest me," said Georgia, "but I tried to do what I was expected to do." At the end of the month she received high grades and thus earned a better spot for her easel, advancing to the intermediate class.

Georgia also studied anatomy. This meant drawing a live model rather than a plaster cast. At that time, men and women took life-drawing classes separately. The teacher, John Vanderpoel, a gentle Dutchman, began the first lesson with a lecture. After a while he said, "Come out," to a curtain Georgia had not noticed before. Georgia was shocked by the man who emerged, "naked except for a small loincloth." Although at home she had gone swimming with boys in skimpy bathing suits, seeing a nude model was different. "He was definitely there to be looked at." She felt embarrassed. "I don't remember learning anything except that I finally became accustomed to the idea of the nude model," she wrote in her autobiography.

Georgia preferred Vanderpoel's lectures on drawing the human figure to her other classes. As he talked, he drew with black and white crayons on large sheets of tan paper. Later his lectures were printed in a book, *The Human Figure*. Georgia bought it and kept it for years. Looking back she said that Vanderpoel was "one of the few real teachers I have known." At the end of the year he ranked her first in the class of twenty-nine women. However, Georgia never developed a strong interest in the human figure as a subject for painting.

In June 1906, Georgia went home to Williamsburg for her summer vacation. There she came down with typhoid fever and was seriously ill for months. By September she had begun to recover, but the illness left her too weak to return to school. Her long straight hair had fallen out due to high fever, and she wore a lace cap to cover her bald head. As she slowly regained her strength, her hair grew back in little curls.

By spring Georgia felt ready to go back out into the world. She decided to apply for a job as a drawing teacher although she had not finished her course of studies. She wrote to the School of the Art Institute of Chicago asking for a letter of recommendation, and one was sent back. But during the summer she changed her mind. Perhaps she was influenced by her teacher and mentor, Mrs. Willis, because she decided to attend the art school where Mrs. Willis had gone.

Georgia O'Keeffe and family, c. 1916. Georgia is in the hammock in white dress and cap.

Eugene Speicher, Portrait of Georgia O'Keeffe, 1908.

Oil paint and turpentine

Traveling once more for the sake of her art, Georgia took a train to New York City in September 1907 and enrolled at the Art Students League. Georgia loved New York. It was crowded, noisy, and full of excitement.

The League featured individual studios, each taught by a painter or sculptor. The minute Georgia stepped inside the building, she was thrilled by the smell of oil paint and turpentine. In the afternoons she took a still life and portrait class with William Merritt Chase, a prominent American painter. "He wore a high silk hat, rather tight fine brown suit, light colored spats and gloves, a carnation in his buttonhole," remembered Georgia. "When he entered the building a rustle seemed to flow from the ground floor to the top that 'Chase has arrived!'"

The students worked in oil imitating Chase's style of vigorous brush strokes and his palette of deep contrasting colors. "Every day we had to paint a new still life." Once a week he came to critique the students' work. The students would quickly pull out their five or six canvases for criticism. The following week the students painted over their previous work. As the weeks went by, the slick canvases had eight or ten paintings layered one on top of the other.

Georgia's fellow students liked her. Everyone affectionately called her "Patsy" because of her Irish last name. She was still full of mischief. Along

William Merritt Chase conducting a class at the Art Students League, New York, 1907.
Georgia is probably one of the students in this photograph.

with other students, she played pranks such as eating the fruit that had been set up for still life class or bringing street musicians into the studio, pushing back the paint-spattered easels, and dancing to the tunes.

Portrait students constantly asked Georgia to pose for them. Eugene Speicher, the class monitor, persisted relentlessly. She kept refusing because it would have meant missing one of her own classes. One day Eugene blocked her way as she headed upstairs to class. He said he wouldn't let her pass until she agreed to pose. "It doesn't matter what you do," he teased. "I'm going to be a great painter, and you will probably end up teaching painting in some girls' school."

Finally he let Georgia go. But when she reached her class she didn't like the model, so she went back to Eugene and sat for him that day and the next. His portrait of "Patsy O'Keeffe" won him a fifty-dollar prize. Today it hangs in the League's Members' Room.

On the second day Georgia was posing for Eugene, a classmate suggested that they all go to see some drawings by Auguste Rodin, a modern French artist, that were being exhibited at 291, a gallery downtown. The teachers at the League had urged the students to see the show, so Georgia and the others took off.

On the way, the men said that they had heard that Alfred Stieglitz, owner of the gallery, was "quite a talker" and they wanted to "get him going."

Stieglitz, a pioneer photographer trained in Berlin, Germany, had devised a way to take dreamy pictures at night and in the rain and snow. As founder of the Photo-Secession movement, he was trying to get photography recognized as a fine art form by museums. To achieve his goal, he organized exhibits of the work of leading photographers as well as the work of avant-garde artists like Rodin, which stirred up debates.

Georgia and her classmates rode an elevator to the top floor and entered a bare room. "Stieglitz came out of a sort of dark place with something photographic in his right hand," said Georgia. "It was dripping water on the floor." He "glared at us from behind his pince-nez glasses." The young men immediately started a heated discussion with him about art, and the talk got "louder and louder till it became quite violent," recalled Georgia. While she waited for her friends, she withdrew and looked at Rodin's drawings. At the time, the drawings seemed like "just a lot of scribbles" to her, but they must have made an impression on her, because years later she would paint a series of nudes in watercolor that are strikingly similar.

At the end of the school year, Georgia won the top still life prize of one hundred dollars for one of her paintings. She also earned a scholarship to study at Amitola, the League's summer school on Lake George in upstate New York. That summer she painted outdoors for the first time.

When she returned home from Lake George, she discovered that her parents had serious financial problems. They could not afford to send her back to the Art Students League. Georgia understood and sympathized with her Papa's "hard luck." Yet without further training, she felt that she could not become an artist. Georgia gave up her dream.

In 1908, two days before she turned twenty-one, Georgia left home again, this time to Chicago, seeking a job to support herself.

Untitled (Rotunda - University of Virginia), 1912–1914.

Something 5
was in the air

In Chicago, Georgia lived with her Aunt Ollie and Uncle Charles again. Using her art background, she found jobs as a freelance illustrator. Because Georgia had learned to paint quickly from her teacher William Merritt Chase, she was able to meet tight deadlines. For one of her assignments she created the Old Dutch Cleanser girl chasing dirt, a symbol still in print. Despite her success, Georgia hated commercial art: drawing pictures to sell products. "I could make a living at it," she wrote, "but it wasn't worth the price."

Two years after arriving in Chicago, she came down with a severe case of measles and the illness weakened her eyes. Unable to draw detailed illustrations anymore, she returned home. Her mother had become sick with tuberculosis and thought that living in a drier climate would improve her condition, so the family moved to Charlottesville, Virginia. The University of Virginia, generally known as U.Va, was located in Charlottesville, and Georgia's mother took in student boarders for income.

During the winter of 1911, Georgia corresponded with one of her boyfriends from the Art Students League. From Paris, the center of the art world, he wrote, "I paint all the time. I should like to have you here." Georgia wrote back that she had given up painting. He replied, "You are and always will be an artist."

Georgia's self-imposed exile from art ended in the spring of 1911. Her former teacher and mentor, Mrs. Willis, took a leave of absence from teaching art at Chatham School and asked Georgia to replace her for six weeks. Georgia accepted the job and liked it. Perhaps she could make a life for herself as an art teacher, she thought.

Meanwhile, her sisters took art courses at U.Va during the summer, the only time women were allowed to attend the school. They excitedly told Georgia about their eccentric teacher, Alon Bement, and persuaded her to visit the class and see for herself.

Bement was an assistant professor of fine arts at Teachers College, Columbia University, in New York. He followed the methods of Arthur Wesley Dow, an artist and professor at Teachers College. Like Dow, Bement stressed the difference between directly copying from nature and composing a pleasing design. Dow had created exercises to help students understand composition: how to organize shapes, lines, and colors in a picture. One exercise involved placing a maple leaf on a seven-inch square and moving it around to see the relationship between positive shapes and negative space. His lesson was: "Filling a space in a beautiful way."

As soon as Georgia met Bement and heard these theories, her desire to make art was rekindled. All of a sudden she grasped the idea of abstraction. A picture did not have to represent anything recognizable. She realized, "art could be a thing of your own."

She enrolled in Bement's most advanced drawing class, and he immediately recognized her talent. At the end of the course, he asked her to be his teaching assistant during the following summer.

To tide her over till then, he offered to help her get work teaching art. Georgia wrote to friends asking if they knew of any job openings. One of her classmates from Chatham who lived in Amarillo, Texas, sent her a telegram saying that the position of drawing supervisor of the Amarillo public schools had just become available. Although Georgia had very limited

experience, Bement wrote a glowing if somewhat exaggerated letter of recommendation, and she was hired.

At the end of August 1912, when Georgia was nearly twenty-five, she
boarded a train for Amarillo. Remembering the stories of the Wild West
that her mother had read to her, she later said in an interview with the *New
Yorker* magazine, "I was very excited about going to Texas, where Billy the
Kid had been."

Amarillo, a frontier town with unpaved roads, enchanted Georgia. She
loved the vast windswept plains and arching sky. "I was beside myself," she
said. "The wind—I didn't even mind the dust. Sometimes when I came back
from walking I would be the color of the road."

Instead of living in a boarding house with other teachers, she stayed at
the Magnolia Hotel. "I didn't want them to know how little I knew!" she said.
Cowboys and gold prospectors were her fellow guests, and she enjoyed
hearing them talk about outlaws and cattle rustlers.

Her job consisted of supervising "drawing and penmanship" for hundreds of students in six schools and sometimes giving art lessons. Although
she didn't know much about teaching, the children responded to her enthu-
siasm. Sometimes they even brought their younger brothers and sisters
to class.

Georgia passed on the lessons she had learned from Dow's theories.
She wanted to get across the idea that "art is important in everyday life,"
she said. "I wanted them to learn . . . that when you buy a pair of shoes . . .
or address a letter or comb your hair, consider it carefully, so that it looks
well." But she couldn't teach the leaf-drawing exercise because there were
no maple leaves in the Amarillo desert. So she had the students draw a
square and put a door in it somewhere—"anything to start them thinking
about how to divide a space."

Georgia told the students that anything could be a good subject for art. One day a boy rode his long-haired pony to school. Georgia and the children heaved the pony onto a table to pose for the class.

The school authorities disapproved of her methods. They insisted she teach from the Prang manual, the very one that she had used as a child. Georgia refused. She objected to having the children copy a sequence of dull pictures. Besides, the books were too expensive. However, the state legislature made the Prang book a requirement, and the school board ordered copies of the book. Furious, Georgia instructed her classes not to use the books. And they didn't.

In the summer of 1914, she again worked with Bement, who urged her to go to New York to get her teaching degree. But neither Georgia nor her parents had enough money to pay for her classes. Then unexpectedly, Aunt Ollie gave her a gift: enough money to pay for her studies for one year.

That fall Georgia enrolled at the School of Practical Arts at Teachers College, Columbia University. She lived around the corner from the school in a small room for four dollars a week. The only decoration in her bare room was a pot of geraniums on the fire escape.

More serious and determined than ever before, she plunged into the exciting art world of New York, buzzing with radical new ideas. She wrote, "Something was in the air."

2   *TEACHER'S MANUAL.*   [BOOK :

DRILL EXERCISES.

Drawing-Book, page A.

OBJECT. Practice for proper position of pupil and of paper: proper pencil-holding; free arm movement from left to right, from top to bottom, and from corner to corner.

Directions to the Teacher. — Before beginning work in the book, show pupils how to hold their pencils for free movement and drawing. Give practice in movement with the pencil from left to right, and see that *each pupil* holds the pencil properly (see Fig. 1, p. xiii), — the same for movement from top to bottom (see Fig. 2, p. xiii), — and from corner to corner (see Figs. 3 and 4, p. xiii). For movement and for drawing count 1, 2, 3, to keep the children together.

Practice. — Open your book at page **A**, and place it well back on the desk. Find and read the points at the left of the page (*o, a, b, c, d, e, f*). How far apart are they? (If necessary, the teacher gives the distance, *one inch*.)

Sit up straight, and with pencil in hand, held properly, begin at point *a*, and move the hand across the page (without drawing and with the whole arm movement) at least three times; then draw lightly across the page with one continuous movement. Repeat the movement and drawing, remembering to hold the pencil properly and to practice the movement before drawing. *No erasing.*

Read the points at the top of the page (*o, 1, 2, 3, etc.*). How far apart are they? Draw from these points down the page, remembering pencil-holding and movement. Draw also from the upper left to the lower right corner, and from the upper right to the lower left corner, with proper pencil-holding and movement. Draw each line with one continuous movement. *No erasing.*

Cover of 291, No. 4, 1915. Art by John Marin.

A woman 6
on paper

At Columbia, Georgia struck up a friendship with Anita Pollitzer, who was also studying to be an art teacher. Anita was twenty, seven years younger than Georgia, and came from an upper-middle class Jewish family in South Carolina. In contrast to Georgia, Anita was small, bubbly, and outgoing.

They first met at the Art Students League where they were both taking a painting and drawing class. Georgia and Anita shared a passion for art and music and spent a great deal of time together.

Often they rode the trolley to see revolutionary paintings from Europe at Stieglitz's gallery, 291. Stieglitz courageously was the first to show the Cubist work of Pablo Picasso and Georges Braque. People were shocked by paintings of geometric forms, depicting many views of a figure or object at once. But Georgia appreciated innovative art, and liked the unusual gallery.

Georgia visited Stieglitz's gallery often. "I didn't understand some of the things he showed, but it was a new wave, I knew that. It showed you how you could make up your mind about what to paint."

At 291 Georgia saw an exhibit of paintings by John Marin, a young American artist. Georgia especially admired Marin's splashes of color and loved a little blue crayon drawing that hung on the door. This time she went up to Stieglitz. She asked him if a particular Marin piece had sold. He told her it had. At that moment, Georgia realized that perhaps she could support herself as a painter.

Bement, her old mentor and supporter, was also back at Columbia. One day she passed his classroom and heard music. Intrigued, Georgia stepped into the room. Bement was playing a phonograph record and asked the students to draw the sounds they heard. Georgia did the exercises, too. Since childhood she had adored music, and the idea of "translating music into something for the eye" excited her.

Bement also introduced her to the work of Wassily Kandinsky, a Russian-born painter. Kandinsky believed that there was a strong connection between visual art and music. He used bold color, lines, and shapes to express inner feelings as abstractions: images that do not represent anything recognizable in the real world. "The artist must have something to say," he wrote, and Georgia never forgot that lesson.

Learning about painting interested her far more than learning about teaching, and her final grades were poor. Nevertheless, Dow recognized her great ability as an artist. In a letter of recommendation, he wrote that Georgia was "one of the most talented people in art that we have ever had."

That summer Bement again invited Georgia to be his assistant at University of Virginia. In June she left New York for Charlottesville. Anita went home to South Carolina and sent Georgia a letter. She told her that, before leaving New York, she had gone to 291 and had asked Stieglitz for an issue of his magazine, *Camera Work*, that contained reproductions of Rodin's drawings.

When Anita, a subscriber, received the number four issue of *291*, the gallery's monthly magazine, the cover featured a drawing by John Marin. She loved it and ordered a copy of the magazine for Georgia as well.

Over the summer in her free time, Georgia kept painting and drawing and frequently sent her work to Anita for comments. Yet she felt
ambivalent. "I always have a curious feeling about some of my things,"
she wrote. "I hate to show them . . . I am afraid people won't understand—and I hope they won't—and am afraid they will."

In her letters, Georgia mentioned a new "very good friend." His
name was Arthur Macmahon, a professor of Political Science at U.Va.
in the summer, and at Columbia University in the winter. Like Georgia,
Arthur enjoyed the outdoors, and they hiked through the mountains.
Along the way, they discussed the war raging in Europe, political theories, and feminism. At that time, 1915, women still did not have the right
to vote. Arthur believed they should. So did Georgia. She and Anita
had already joined the National Woman's Party to campaign for the
women's suffrage movement, as the fight for women's right to vote was
called.

Although Georgia claimed that she and Arthur were just good
friends, when he left at the end of the summer, she missed him terribly
and began writing to him.

In September she faced a difficult decision. Should she go to New
York and look for a job (and be near Arthur), or should she accept an
offer to teach at Columbia College for women in South Carolina? Reluctantly, Georgia accepted the teaching position because she only had to
give four classes a week and would have more time for painting.

But she found the environment stifling. There was no interest in
art and ideas. Georgia cheered herself up by taking long walks alone
and gathering colorful fall flowers for her dorm room. And as she had
hoped, her "hibernation," as she called it, did indeed give her time to
paint. To keep in touch with the art world, Georgia subscribed to 291

No. 17 Special, 1919.

and eagerly read Anita's news of shows at the gallery. She wrote to Anita, "I believe I would rather have Stieglitz like something—anything I had done—than anyone else I know of."

One day in October, she hung her most recent work on the wall of her studio and studied it critically. "I could see how each painting or drawing had been done according to one teacher or another, and said to myself, 'I have things in my head that are not like what anyone has taught me—shapes and ideas.'"

Georgia realized that she had acquired the skill to use art materials. "But what to say with them?" she wrote. "I guess if I'm going to do something that is my own, I'd better start, and I'll start in black and white."

On that day, she put away her watercolors, oils, and pastels and feverishly began a series of abstract charcoal drawings. "It was like learning to walk," she remembered. Every night she spread rough paper on the floor and crawled around, drawing with charcoal. "I was alone and singularly free," she wrote, "no one to satisfy but myself."

At Thanksgiving when she had just turned twenty-eight, Arthur visited her, and she spent a few wonderful days with him. After he left, she felt lonely and confused. Her friendship with him had deepened to love, and she expressed her intense emotions on paper. "I just exploded it into the picture," she wrote. "It was what I wanted to tell him but I didn't dare in words."

During the Christmas holiday, she felt tempted to see him in New York. Instead she stayed at the empty college and kept drawing her "Special" series. By the end of December, Georgia bundled up a batch of her new work and sent it to Anita with instructions not to show the drawings to anyone.

The cardboard tube arrived, and Anita opened it on Saturday, January 1, 1916. She was astounded. "These drawings were saying something that had not yet been said," she recalled. "I knew after looking at them that there was one person who must see them."

Disobeying Georgia's orders, she wrapped up the drawings and took them with her to a matinee of the play *Peter Pan*. When the performance ended, Anita hurried downtown to 291. The elevator was broken, so she climbed up four flights of stairs to the gallery. Stieglitz was alone. Anita asked him if he would like to see what she had under her arm.

She unrolled the charcoal drawings and spread them out on the floor. "He looked...he looked again...the room was quiet. "Then he smiled and said to Anita, "You say a woman did these?"

"Yes," she answered.

Stieglitz said, "Well, tell her they're the purest, finest, sincerest things that have entered 291 in a long while...I think I will give these drawings a show."

Then he exclaimed, "Finally a woman on paper!"

Georgia O'Keeffe in Canyon, Texas, 1916–1917, photograph by Alfred Stieglitz.

Painting what I Feel

7

Anita excitedly wrote to Georgia and told her what she had done with the "Special" drawings, quoting Stieglitz as well.

Georgia responded, "There seems to be nothing for me to say except Thank you.—I could hardly believe my eyes when I read your letter this afternoon." Then she added, "If Stieglitz says any more about them—ask him why he liked them."

About a week later, Georgia wrote to Stieglitz and asked him herself.

He replied, "My dear Miss O'Keeffe, It is impossible for me to put into words what I saw and felt in your drawings . . . I do want to tell you that they gave me much joy. They were a real surprise . . . If at all possible I would like to show them, but we will see about that . . . The future is rather hazy, but the present is very positive and delightful."

Georgia repeated that last sentence in a letter to Anita. She liked Stieglitz's attitude toward life, which matched her own, and that mattered to her even more than the possibility of a show.

On January 5, 1916, Georgia unexpectedly received an offer to head the art department at West Texas Normal College in Canyon, Texas. As a condition of accepting the position, she would have to return to Columbia

Alfred Stieglitz, 1902, photograph by Gertrude Käsebier.

University and take Dow's spring term class "Methods of Teaching Art." Of course, being in New York would also mean seeing Arthur. Georgia set off.

Soon after Georgia arrived in New York, Arthur proposed marriage. Although she still had strong feelings for him, she did not become engaged. Arthur didn't care about art the way she did, and she was dedicated to her work.

One day that spring while Georgia was eating lunch in the Columbia University cafeteria, another student came up to her and asked, "Are you Virginia O'Keeffe?"

"No," said Georgia. "Why?"

"Well," the woman went on, "it says on the bulletin board that Virginia O'Keeffe is having an exhibition at a gallery called 291."

Georgia immediately realized the drawings were hers. Stieglitz had mixed up her first name with the state where she had lived. Even though she had known he might show her work, she was "startled and shocked" that he had done so without her consent.

Annoyed, she stormed down to the gallery to confront Stieglitz, who happened to be away on jury duty. Georgia wandered through the exhibit and calmed down a little as she saw her work displayed in a beautiful space along with watercolors and oils by two other little-known artists.

The next week she returned to 291 and asked Stieglitz, "Who gave you permission to hang these drawings?"

"No one," he said.

"You will have to take them down," she said.

"I think you are mistaken," said Stieglitz.

"Well, I made the drawings. I am Georgia O'Keeffe."

Stieglitz was amused, interested, and charmed. "You don't know what you've done in these pictures," he said.

"Certainly I know what I've done," she shot back. "Do you think I'm an idiot?"

Unperturbed, he kept talking. Gradually Georgia began to trust him and felt somewhat exhilarated that he understood her work. The drawings remained on the wall through May, June, and July, and Stieglitz said, "They created a sensation."

Then one day in early May, Georgia received a call that her mother had died suddenly from tuberculosis. That night she took a train to Charlottesville to be with her family. Her grief brought her closer than ever to her sisters. For the next six weeks, Georgia felt depressed and disinterested in everything, even art.

By the end of June, though, her spirits lifted, and she took a summer position teaching at U.Va. She resumed drawing in charcoal, then black watercolor. Finally, she felt ready for color and used blue watercolor to create the abstract painting *Blue Lines*.

At the end of August, Georgia left Virginia for a new job in Canyon, Texas, a small town near Amarillo. The teachers' training college was open to men and women. To her delight she was the only art teacher and could do exactly as she pleased. She gave classes in drawing, costume design, interior decoration, and the teaching of drawing. Georgia taught art as a way of seeing.

The students admired her unusual ways. As always, Georgia's clothes attracted attention. "Oh, she wore black," remembered one of her students. "Black, black, black! And her clothing was like men's clothing. Straight lines . . . she didn't believe in lace . . . or ruffles or things like that."

When Georgia first arrived, she stayed in another teacher's house. But the rose-patterned wallpaper drove her crazy. "I moved the next day," she wrote. She ultimately rented a room in a bungalow belonging to physics teacher Douglas Shirley. His wife, Mrs. Shirley, worried that the room was bare and had no curtains, but Georgia preferred it that way.

Townspeople thought Georgia was strange because on Sundays, instead of going to church, she took long walks by herself on the prairie. Herds of cattle had been driven across the plains and some had died, their carcasses bleached in the sun. To Georgia the bones had extraordinary beauty. She brought them to class to share with the students. The images of the bones stayed with her and were to become a major theme in her painting years later.

Before her mother died, Georgia had promised that she would take care of her youngest sister, Claudie. Their father was often away from home looking for work. So seventeen-year-old Claudie went to live with Georgia and attended West Texas State Normal College. Sometimes Georgia and Claudie hiked over to Palo Duro Canyon, twenty miles away. The landscape enthralled Georgia and inspired about fifty paintings. She wrote to Anita, "Tonight I walked into the sunset . . . the whole sky—was just blazing."

Most people didn't understand Georgia's painting. Once she showed an image of the canyon to her landlady, Mrs. Shirley. Mrs. Shirley said, "It doesn't look like the canyon to me," and Georgia explained it was how she *felt* about the canyon. Mrs. Shirley joked that Georgia must have had a stomachache when she painted it.

During this year in Texas, Georgia kept exchanging letters with Arthur. He sent her books by philosophers and a subscription to *New Republic*, a political magazine he thought she would find interesting.

Stieglitz, as she referred to him, sent books and letters as well. "I'm enjoying his letters so much—learning to know him," Georgia wrote to Anita. Sometimes Georgia rolled up her recent work in newspapers and mailed

No. 22 - Special, 1916/1917.

them to Stieglitz. In December 1916, he included some of her drawings in a group show. Anita went to see the exhibit and was thrilled for Georgia. "You're hanging with [John] Marin," she wrote. "I call this important, and I know I'm right."

She was.

In April 1917, when Georgia was twenty-nine years old, Stieglitz gave her her first solo exhibition. It featured her Texas landscapes and blue watercolors. She said, "The first picture I ever sold was from that show. It was a black shape with smoke above it, a picture of the early morning train roaring in."

When the school semester ended in late May, Georgia was tempted to go to New York for a few days before starting to teach the summer session in Canyon. The trip would cost two hundred dollars, which was all the money she had saved. She withdrew her savings from the bank and rode the train to New York the next morning.

The city looked different. In April the United States had entered World War I. Soldiers in uniform filled the streets, and colorful flags of the Allies (Great Britain, France, Russia, and the United States) fluttered along Fifth Avenue.

When Georgia walked into 291, the walls were bare. Stieglitz had taken down the show of her artwork because the gallery was closing for good. But he hung the entire exhibition again just for her and took photographs of her standing in front of it. "This was the first time Stieglitz photographed me," she recalled. He only took pictures of people who moved him, and he was fascinated by what he called her Mona Lisa smile and her graceful hands.

Georgia O'Keeffe, 1918, photograph by Alfred Stieglitz.

Evening Star VI, 1917.

Georgia returned to West Texas Normal College to teach. In a letter to Anita she wrote, "My summer work here is great." In her private life, though, Georgia felt indecisive. During her short visit to New York she had met Paul Strand, a young photographer. Georgia loved his work, and she liked Paul. As soon as she returned to Canyon, they began writing to each other.

In the meantime, another man was pursuing her. Ted Reid, an older student at the college and a Texan, appreciated her feeling for the landscape. During the summer, Ted drove her out to the country so that she could sketch and watch the sunset. They walked on the prairie day and night. Soon he proposed. Georgia turned him down.

Juggling romances did not distract Georgia from painting. That summer she created powerful abstractions in watercolor expressing her feelings about nature. She recalled how she and Claudie took long walks away from town in the late afternoon. "The evening star would be high in the sunset sky when it was still broad daylight," she wrote. "That evening star fascinated me." Inspired, she made ten watercolors of the star.

Georgia also painted *Starlight Night*. Skillfully, she left patches of the paper unpainted to suggest flickering stars.

She sent her new work to Stieglitz and it thrilled him. He described the watercolors to a friend as "a few wonders." Although he had closed his gallery, he worked at arranging exhibitions for other galleries. He devoted much of his time to guiding Georgia's blossoming career. "She is the spirit of 291," he wrote.

Georgia and Claudie planned a trip to Colorado that August. But that year heavy rains had washed out bridges, so there was no direct train. "If you can't go straight, go crooked," Georgia said. Their alternative route took them to Santa Fe, New Mexico, where they stopped for a few days. The adobe town and clear, dry desert air delighted Georgia. She said, "I loved it immediately. From then on, I was always on my way back."

Upon returning to Canyon in the fall, she found that the mood on campus had changed. With the war raging, patriotic spirits ran high. Her own youngest brother, Alexis, had enlisted in the army. Georgia encouraged her students to complete school first.

The talk about war depressed Georgia. She stopped making art. And she felt differently about teaching. Some members of the faculty and townspeople accused her of being unpatriotic. When a shopkeeper displayed Christmas cards with a strong anti-German message, Georgia asked him to remove the cards. They were "certainly not in keeping with any Christmas spirit I ever heard of," she wrote to Elizabeth, Stieglitz's niece. Georgia and Elizabeth had struck up a friendship when Georgia was in New York.

At about the same time, Claudie left Canyon to begin teaching in Spur, Texas. That winter the weather turned bitterly cold. Because of the war, there was a shortage of coal for Georgia's potbellied stove. She stuffed paper into the top of her dress to stay warm as she braved the icy wind on the walk from her room to the college. In January 1918, she came down with the flu. A flu epidemic was sweeping the country, and thousands died. By the middle of February, Georgia was too sick to teach and asked the school for a short leave of absence. A rumor spread that she had been forced to leave permanently because of her antiwar sentiments.

Stieglitz was deeply concerned about her, and his heartfelt letters urging her to return to New York moved her to tears. Instead, as soon as she was strong enough to travel, Georgia went to stay with Leah Harris, a former teacher at the college in Canyon. Leah now lived on a farm in Waring, Texas. For the next few months on Leah's farm, Georgia slowly regained her strength and began painting again. During this time she also wrote regularly to Stieglitz and sent him new paintings. He insisted she come to New York. But she was considering returning to Canyon to teach summer school. Stieglitz feared for her health. "I want her to live—I never wanted anything as much as that," he wrote to Paul Strand.

Both men cared about her. Her relationship with Strand had cooled, however, and she was growing closer to Stieglitz. "He is probably more necessary to me than anyone I know," she wrote to Elizabeth. Elizabeth offered to let Georgia stay in her studio if she came to New York.

Stieglitz and Strand worriedly discussed Georgia's situation. In May 1918, Stieglitz, who didn't like to travel, gave Strand the money for train tickets and sent him to Texas to get Georgia. Reluctant to give up her independence, Georgia nevertheless realized how much she depended on Stieglitz. At last on June 8, coughing and feverish, she left with Strand.

On June 10 they arrived in New York at dawn. Stieglitz met them at the train station and swept Georgia away to Elizabeth's studio. The most important thing in the world to him was Georgia. He visited her every day.

And to Elizabeth he wrote, "It all seems like a fairy story." Stieglitz, age fifty-four, and Georgia, age thirty, had fallen in love.

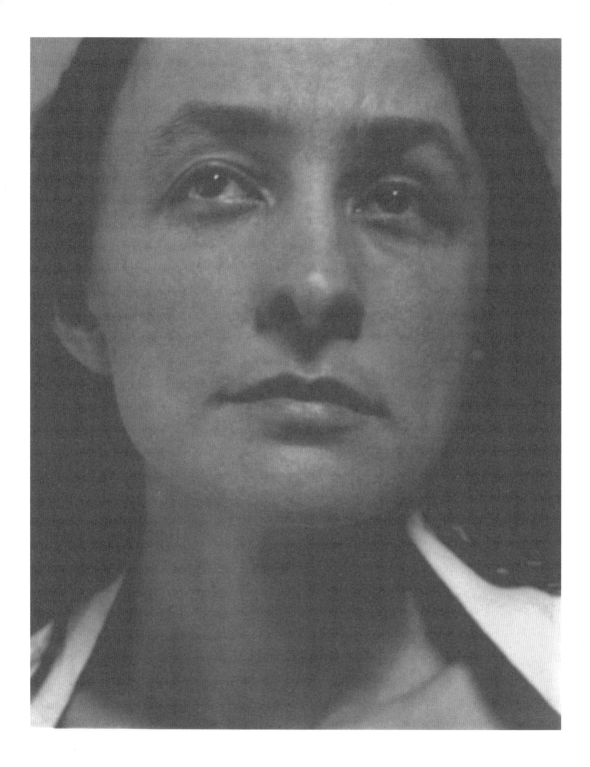

Painting 9 her joy

Georgia liked Elizabeth's bright, cheery studio at the top of a brownstone. She stayed in the front room that had pale yellow walls and an orange floor. Georgia put her bed under the skylight so that she could look up and see the stars at night.

The small back room was dark, and Stieglitz used it for developing photographs. Every day he came over to look after her and asked one of his brothers, a doctor, to treat her. Slowly Georgia became well.

Stieglitz had been unhappily married for nearly twenty-five years to Emmeline, a woman more interested in fashion and society than art. He moved out of their apartment and asked for a divorce.

By July, Stieglitz moved into the studio with Georgia. In those days it was scandalous for a man and woman to live together without being married, especially because Stieglitz was still legally married to someone else. But Georgia didn't care. She and Stieglitz loved each other. As artists, they respected and inspired each other. "Each of us was really interested in what the other was doing," she said.

He began to photograph her in a series of portraits that eventually numbered three hundred prints. She wore no makeup and didn't even check her appearance in a mirror before posing. Georgia had never thought she was beautiful. She especially hated her dimples. "You see, I'd never known what I looked like or thought about it much," she said. "I was amazed to find

Georgia O'Keeffe, 1919, photograph by Alfred Stieglitz.

my face was lean and structured. I'd always thought it was round." Later she said that in his pictures, "I can see myself, and it has helped me to say what I want to say—in paint."

In the studio, she created a series of abstractions in oil, *Music, Pink and Blue*, that glowed with luscious colors, revealing her joy. As happy as she was, she still expected to go back to Canyon, Texas, in the fall to teach.

Then one day, Stieglitz asked her what she would do if she could do anything she wanted for a year. "I promptly said I would like to have a year to paint," said Georgia. "He thought for a while and then remarked that he thought he could arrange that."

Stieglitz had made similar arrangements for other struggling artists. He approached a client who agreed to advance a thousand dollars for Georgia's work. At that time, unknown artists like her usually received two or three hundred dollars at most for a painting. When Georgia heard the news, she quickly submitted her resignation to the college in Canyon and sent for her things. "They came in a barrel and among them were all my old drawings and paintings," she wrote. "I put them in with the wastepaper trash to throw away and that night when Stieglitz and I came home after dark the paintings and drawings were blowing all over the street. We left them there and went in."

That summer Stieglitz's widowed mother, Hedwig, told him to bring Georgia to the family's vacation home, Oaklawn, on Lake George in upstate New York. Hedwig had never liked Stieglitz's wife because she treated him poorly. Now Hedwig welcomed Georgia to the family. The Stieglitzes were Jewish and originally from Germany. They were a big, talkative clan. At the dinner table, there were usually eighteen to twenty people. They ate three big meals a day, with tea and cakes served in the late afternoon. "Four times as much food as anyone could eat," said Georgia, who was used to a

Music - Pink and Blue II, 1919.

light diet. The house itself, crammed with knickknacks and overstuffed furniture, appalled her.

Nevertheless she enjoyed herself at Lake George and wrote, "I was never so happy in my life." Georgia and Stieglitz took off by themselves and went rowing, swimming, and walking. Members of the family observed how much the two loved each other.

Georgia had brought oils and watercolors, and spent many hours painting. Stieglitz took pictures of her sitting outdoors on the ground, working in watercolor with a Japanese brush. Her series of canna lilies in vivid red expressed her intense pleasure. "I know I cannot paint a flower," she wrote later, "but maybe in terms of paint color I can convey to you my experience of the flower." These were the first of her single-flower paintings.

When fall turned to winter, she and Stieglitz went back to the studio in New York. In November Georgia suffered two painful shocks. Her father had fallen from a steep roof while working and had died. And a month after the war ended on November 11, her brother Alexis came back from France on a stretcher. His heart and lungs had been severely injured by mustard gas, a chemical weapon used by the Germans.

Despite her sorrows, Georgia welcomed her new life with Stieglitz. They followed a routine of working during the day and going out for dinner at night dressed in matching black capes and hats. The studio had no kitchen, but Georgia did not want to be bothered cooking anyway. On Saturdays they ate with a few artist friends at the Far East Tea Garden, an inexpensive Chinese restaurant. Georgia was the only woman present and usually kept quiet as the men discussed topics such as the meaning of art. "I knew I could paint as well as some of them who were sitting around talking," she recalled.

Soon she would prove it.

Georgia O'Keeffe, 1920/1922, photograph by Alfred Stieglitz.

House and Trees, Lake George, 1932, photograph by Alfred Stieglitz.

One hundred 10
mona lisas

While Georgia and Stieglitz were both passionate about art, as people they were quite different. She needed solitude, he thrived on company. She wanted a baby. He said, "You'll never be able to paint if you have a child about."

During the next few years, their differences remained unresolved as their lives followed a pattern. Every summer they went to Lake George. The family's big summer house had been sold because it was too expensive to maintain. Stieglitz, the eldest son, took charge of renovating a smaller place on the property called the Farmhouse. Georgia enthusiastically painted furniture, washed floors, and planted a vegetable garden. Gardening rekindled pleasant memories of her childhood on the farm in Wisconsin. "The growing corn was one of my special interests," she wrote, "the light colored veins of the dark green leaves reaching out in opposite directions."

Once the Farmhouse was settled, Georgia felt ready to start painting. But the Farmhouse swarmed with noisy relatives. Georgia never allowed company when she was painting, and wouldn't even show a picture to Stieglitz until it was finished. She required privacy. On a hill farthest from the lake she discovered an old cow shed and decided to fix it up as a studio. Stieglitz's newly married niece, Elizabeth, and her bridegroom pitched in and helped. Together they replaced the shingles with tar paper, laid the floor, and oiled the rafters. In late August the Shanty, as Georgia called it, was ready. She set up her easel, neatly squeezed globs of oil paint on her milk glass palette, and painted her first picture there. "A good one!" exclaimed Stieglitz when she showed it to him.

From then on, the Shanty belonged to Georgia. She even painted a portrait of it. Apples became another favorite subject. One day Georgia invited the wife of one of Stieglitz's nephews to paint green apples with her. At noon they left the Shanty to have lunch. When they came back they found a cow wandering inside; it had eaten the apples and knocked over Georgia's palette. With peals of laughter they shooed out the mooing cow.

That summer Georgia produced a series of still lifes including plums, pears, and avocados. She did landscapes of Lake George with the hills beyond, and in the autumn, purple and flaming red leaves. Sometimes she tied a wooden tray around her waist to hold brushes and paint, and did preliminary studies outdoors. For her, it was a period of great productivity. For Stieglitz too. Many days they both worked fifteen hours straight.

When the weather turned cold they went back to New York. Because their building was going to be gutted for remodeling, they had to move. Stieglitz's brother Lee, the doctor who had treated Georgia, invited them to stay at his house on East Sixty-fifth Street. They settled there in the spring of 1920.

By July, Georgia needed to get away by herself and took a trip to York Beach, Maine. She stayed at an inn owned by friends of the Stieglitzes and loved her cozy room overlooking the ocean. During the day she roamed the sandy beach and collected shells to study for still life paintings. At night she watched the beam of light from the Cape Neddick Light Station. She wrote to Stieglitz suggesting that they buy a house in York Beach. He had no interest in going to Maine or any place other than his beloved Lake George. "I'm a real stick-in-the-mud," he said.

Apple Family – 2, 1920.

Two Pink Shells / Pink Shell, 1937.

Georgia came home refreshed but convinced she would return to Maine. At Lake George, she continued to work in oils, pastels, and water colors, while Stieglitz took more photographs. By the following winter he felt prepared to exhibit his pictures. Since the building that had housed gallery 291 had been torn down, he showed his work at the Anderson Galleries on Park Avenue. The exhibit of one hundred photographs included forty-five of Georgia. Some showed her standing in front of her own drawings and paintings. Others portrayed her in the nude. Thousands of curious viewers crowded the gallery.

To Georgia's surprise and indignation, she attracted attention as a model. People wanted to meet her. Art critic Henry McBride wrote, "Mona Lisa got but one portrait of herself worth talking about. O'Keeffe got a hundred." That number wasn't correct, but he was right that Georgia had become a "personality."

Critics and friends admired the beauty and richness of Stieglitz's new work. The Museum of Fine Arts, Boston, bought a group of the pictures, a first in the history of photography. But Georgia objected to being cast as Stieglitz's divine inspiration like a goddess. She felt that reviewers were falsely idealizing her.

Eventually Georgia calmed down and realized that publicity was a necessary part of becoming recognized as an artist. "Most people buy pictures more through their ears than their eyes," she wrote. "So one must be written about and talked about whether one likes it or not."

Calla Lily Turned Away, 1923.

Georgia 11
blooming

Georgia and Stieglitz had mixed feelings about selling their work. She needed to make a living. He lived on a small inheritance. As a gallery owner and representative of young American painters and photographers, he never took a commission for a sale. He wanted to protect "his" artists and wouldn't even lend their pictures to museums that had not bought them. When a collector wanted to buy one of Georgia's paintings, he was reluctant to part with it unless he thought the buyer truly appreciated the quality of the work and would give it a good home.

By 1923, Stieglitz thought it was time for Georgia to have another show. In those days it was rare for a woman to be recognized as a serious artist, especially an American who had never studied in Europe. She said, "All the male artists I knew, of course, made it very plain that as a woman I couldn't make it—I might as well stop painting." This attitude made her more determined than ever to succeed.

Her large solo exhibition opened in January 1923 at the Anderson Galleries. About five hundred people jammed the place every day. Georgia said the room was so crowded you could hardly get inside. The show included examples of everything she had done since 1916, from abstract charcoal drawings and watercolors to new paintings of apples, calla lilies, and corn. Twenty pieces were sold, many to family members and friends.

Again, Henry McBride, the art critic, gave the exhibition a rave review. Of her work he wrote, "It represents a great stride, particularly for an American. The result is a calmness."

McBride's comments pleased Georgia. However, around this time an art magazine had published an article stating that there were no great women artists. Women could only be creative by having children. Stieglitz debunked this pseudo-scientific theory. "Women can . . . produce art," he declared, "and Georgia O'Keeffe is the proof of it."

But Georgia still wanted a child. Stieglitz adamantly opposed the idea. His daughter Kitty had suffered a serious depression requiring psychiatric care after childbirth. And his favorite sister had died in childbirth. But Georgia's sister Catherine, on the other hand, had a baby girl and was fine. Finally, Georgia gave in to his wishes and the matter was closed. From that point on, their pictures were their children.

Still the decision left her feeling sad, and she again retreated to Maine. Stieglitz hated the separation but respected her need to get away. When she returned to Lake George she energetically produced three canvases in five days, which he pronounced as "All A1."

The following year Georgia painted her first gigantic flower. She was inspired by a quiet still life by nineteenth-century artist Henri Fantin-Latour that she saw at a museum. To her the delicacy of a tiny flower in the painting contrasted with the size, noise, and hectic pace of New York. She said, "I realized that were I to paint the same flowers so small, no one would look at them . . . So I thought, 'I'll make them big like the huge buildings going up.'"

When she allowed Stieglitz to see her first large flower, he stood in the doorway and said, "Well, Georgia, I don't know how you're going to get away with anything like that—you aren't planning to show it, are you?"

She was. And she was going to do more.

Calla Lily in Tall Glass – No. 2, 1923.

There were other big changes that year. In September, Stieglitz's wife finally granted him a divorce. Now he was free to marry Georgia. At first she refused. As far as she was concerned things were fine the way they were. What's more, she didn't want to give up her independence and become a Stieglitz. In those days, a married woman typically took her husband's last name. Georgia wanted to keep hers. She was thirty-seven years old and had established herself as a professional artist.

But she dearly loved Stieglitz and eventually agreed to marry him. On December 11, 1924, they took a ferry to New Jersey and were married by a justice of the peace.

In the months following their marriage when someone addressed her as Mrs. Stieglitz she snapped, "I am Georgia O'Keeffe. I've had a hard time hanging on to my name, but I hang on to it with my teeth."

Georgia O'Keeffe and Alfred Stieglitz at Lake George, 1929.

The Shelton with Sunspots, NY, 1926.

I did it anyway 12

One day in 1925, Georgia went walking on Park Avenue and saw a sky-scraper going up at Forty-ninth Street and Lexington Avenue: the Shelton Hotel. She and Stieglitz needed to find a place to live, because his brother Lee had sold the brownstone where they had been staying. Georgia decided to try the Shelton. The manager took her up in the elevator and showed her two rooms on the thirtieth floor, the very top of the building. "I had never lived up so high before," she wrote, "and was so excited that I began talking about trying to paint New York. Of course, I was told that it was an impossible idea—even the men hadn't done too well with it. But I did it anyway."

She chose an apartment in the northeast corner of the Shelton overlooking the East River. Gargoyles jutted out above the windows. There were no curtains to obscure the views. The walls of the rooms were painted pale gray, and the furniture was covered in off-white fabric. Georgia insisted on a plain, uncluttered environment for her work.

Wearing an apron over her black dress, Georgia painted at an easel in natural light coming through the window. She used a separate brush for each color to keep them from getting muddied. One painting in silvery blues shows a tugboat puffing along the East River and billows of smoke curling from smokestacks on the shore. She developed paintings from pencil sketches. The idea for *The Shelton with Sunspots* occurred to her one morning when she went out for a walk before starting to work. Georgia saw the "optical illusion of a bite out of one side of the tower made by the sun."

Another skyscraper that fascinated her was the Radiator Building on Forty-second Street. Georgia's dramatic painting depicts it at night in deep purples, blues, and warm blacks to contrast with the brightly lit windows. A red neon sign on the building usually flashed the words "Scientific American," but she affectionately wrote the name "Stieglitz" in its place.

During the next few years, Georgia did a series of city scenes. In 1926 the first of these paintings was shown in Intimate Gallery, a corner room of Anderson Galleries that Stieglitz had rented. Here, he showed Georgia's work and the paintings and photographs of "his" artists such as Paul Strand, Arthur Dove, and John Marin. Georgia demanded that her painting *City Night* be hung on a wall between two windows. The day the show opened it was the first painting sold, for the sum of twelve hundred dollars, a great deal of money in those days. "The boys," as she called the men painters in Stieglitz's circle, were impressed. Sarcastically she recalled, "From then on they *let* me paint New York."

Meanwhile, she continued developing her series of gigantic flowers. She said to herself, "I will make even busy New Yorkers take time to see what I see of flowers."

New Yorkers did take the time to look. And they were surprised and ecstatic. A reviewer in *New Yorker* magazine wrote, "One O'Keeffe hung in the Grand Central Station would even halt the home-going commuters."

In Georgia's *Red Poppy*, the brilliant petals push beyond the edges of the canvas. *Oriental Poppies, White Larkspur and Roses, Purple and Black Petunias* burst with life. Georgia had planted a bed of dark blue and purple petunias at Lake George so that when they bloomed she could closely study the hues.

Radiator Building – Night, New York, 1927.

Women responded wildly to her art. Critic McBride wrote, "There were more feminine shrieks and screams in the vicinity of O'Keeffe's work this year than ever before."

Once, Georgia invited Dorothy Brett, an English painter, to privately see the show with her on a Sunday morning when the gallery was closed. Georgia and Brett brought more paintings up from the storeroom and propped them against the walls. Brett said, "The whole room blazed and quivered with color—it was shockingly beautiful."

Meanwhile, Georgia's longtime friend Anita Pollitzer had become an officer in the National Woman's Party (NWP), which was founded in 1913 to fight for women's rights. Anita asked Georgia to speak at an NWP dinner in Washington, D.C. Although a bill had been passed in 1920 giving women the right to vote, few became active in government or ran for political office. When Georgia spoke to the five hundred guests, she urged women to try to develop their abilities and earn their own livings.

By this time, Georgia was supporting herself as a painter. She had a show every year after Christmas at the Intimate Gallery. In 1927 she exhibited thirty-six new paintings, and half a dozen of them were sold within the first few days for a total of seventeen thousand dollars.

Much to Stieglitz's displeasure, an anonymous American who lived in France offered to buy six small calla lily panels that Georgia had painted in 1923. Stieglitz mistrusted the motives of this mysterious buyer. Since he didn't want to sell the paintings, he named an outrageous price of twenty-five thousand dollars, the equivalent of two hundred thousand dollars today. The buyer agreed. Stieglitz was shocked. He made the buyer promise to hang the paintings in his home and never to sell them in his lifetime.

The sale made front-page news. *The New York Evening Graphic* printed a picture of Georgia with the headline: "She painted the lily and got $25,000 and fame for doing it!"

Georgia hated the publicity. Stieglitz loved it. From his point of view, France was at last coming to America to buy art. Georgia detested articles that called her an overnight success. Reluctantly she agreed to a few interviews and told one reporter, "Success doesn't come with painting one picture. It is building step by step, against great odds."

Upset by all the commotion, she fled again to Maine. But in May, she returned to New York to leave for Lake George with Stieglitz. That summer the Brooklyn Museum, which already owned some of her work, devoted an entire room to an exhibit of her paintings. And the new Museum of Modern Art in Manhattan invited her to participate in its second show scheduled for late 1929, along with other important American artists.

Praise and commitments pressured her. "It's much more difficult to go on now than it was before," said Georgia. "Every year I have to carry the thing I do enough further so that people are surprised again."

Corn No. 2, 1924.

My world 13

By May 1928, Georgia knew every hill, tree, and leaf at Lake George. "I look around and wonder what one might paint," she wrote to McBride. "Here I feel smothered with green." Georgia needed a fresh subject.

In July she went to Wisconsin to see her aunts and sister Catherine. Visiting family revived good memories of growing up on the farm, and she did a painting of a barn.

Upon returning to Lake George in August, Georgia and Stieglitz spent a few quiet weeks together. Then he suffered a heart attack. Georgia devoted her time to taking care of him, preparing special foods, and screening calls and visitors. Stieglitz felt guilty about keeping her from painting, but he depended on her and appreciated her dedication.

That winter they returned to New York, and she painted very little. The annual exhibit of her work had few new paintings and received lukewarm reviews. Around this time, her friend Dorothy Brett came to New York. She introduced Georgia and Stieglitz to Mabel Dodge Luhan and Mabel's husband, Tony, a Pueblo Indian. They all lived in Taos, New Mexico, and invited Georgia and Stieglitz to come and visit.

Steiglitz didn't want to travel. But Georgia began to dream of going West. She was forty-one years old and longed to return to a part of the country that she adored. She started to plan a trip with Paul Strand's wife,

Beck, who modeled for Stieglitz and had become a friend of Georgia's. Stieglitz hated to let Georgia go, yet he understood her need as an artist. She worried about leaving him. "Going west was the hardest decision I ever had to make," she said. At last she packed a trunk with her paints, brushes, and canvases, and she and Beck set out for New Mexico.

In Santa Fe they rented rooms at a cheap hotel and bought tickets to a San Felipe Indian Corn Dance. At the Corn Dance they bumped into Mabel and Tony Luhan who insisted that they come and stay at their ranch in Taos.

Taos, a small town on a mesa, a flat-topped land formation seven thousand feet high, exhilarated Georgia. She loved the dry, clean air, intense light, and adobe houses made of clay-and-straw bricks. When she first arrived she kept saying, "Well! Well! Well! This is wonderful. No one told me it was like *this*!"

On the ranch, Georgia and Beck stayed in a cottage called Casa Rosita, the Pink House. Georgia had her own studio that overlooked sage-filled plains. She wrote, "In the evening, with the sun at your back, it looks like an ocean, like water . . . the blue-green of the sage and the mountains, the wildflowers in bloom. It's a different kind of color from any I'd ever seen."

To her sister Catherine she wrote, "Lake George is not really painting country. Out here, half your work is done for you."

Almost as soon as she arrived in Taos, Georgia started learning how to drive so that she could explore the countryside. In those days, tourists in New Mexico didn't need a driver's license. The main thing was not to hit a cow or horse roaming along the road. Georgia bought a black Model A Ford with earnings from one of her paintings and named the car "Hello."

One day Georgia went driving with a friend of Mabel's. He took her to Abiquiu, a tiny village at the foot of rocky hills in the Chama River Valley. The only inhabitants at that time were Indians and Spanish-speaking

Georgia O'Keeffe—After Return from New Mexico, 1929, photograph by Alfred Stieglitz.

people. On that excursion, her friend pointed out a place called Ghost Ranch, but they couldn't find a road down through the dense sage. Glimpsing the landscape from above, Georgia remarked, "This is my world, but how to get into it?"

That summer at one of Mabel's numerous gatherings, Georgia met a young photographer, Ansel Adams, who was there taking pictures for the Sierra Club, and Frieda Lawrence, widow of the well-known novelist D. H. Lawrence.

Frieda said, "In late summers we would go camping together and would sleep out so that she could begin to paint early, catching the morning lights. Often after breakfast over our outdoor fire, she would paint the whole day."

At night Georgia would stretch out on a long carpenter's bench beneath a huge pine tree. "I often lay on that bench looking up into the tree—past the trunk and up into the branches," she wrote. "It was particularly fine at night with the stars above the tree." Later Georgia painted that view from memory and titled the picture *The Lawrence Tree*. To see it the way she did, one has to tilt the picture sideways, as though gazing upward. It was one of her favorite paintings.

Georgia also felt inspired to paint more flowers. A white desert flower that bloomed outside her door captivated her. "The large White Flower with the golden heart is something I have to say about White," she wrote. "Whether the flower or the color is the focus I do not know . . . Color is one of the great things in the world that makes life worth living to me."

While she was in Taos, Georgia corresponded with Stieglitz daily. He was glad that she was having such a wonderful summer, but he feared that she would never return. She had planned on going home in July but postponed her departure. Finally, by late August she packed her things and shipped her paintings to New York. "I knew I would have to go back to my Stieglitz," she wrote.

At Lake George they had a happy reunion. Georgia had left Hello in Taos for one of her friends to sell. Now she bought another Ford. Although Georgia thought that Stieglitz might disapprove of her driving, he was charmed and photographed her with the car.

When Georgia and Stieglitz returned to the Shelton in November, a somber mood pervaded the city. New Yorkers were panicking. The stock market had crashed in October 1929, businesses were going bankrupt, and the whole country was plunged into the Great Depression. Nevertheless,

D.H. Lawrence Pine Tree, 1929.

Georgia's paintings continued to sell, and Stieglitz planned her next annual exhibit. He had opened a new gallery, An American Place, on Madison Avenue. Georgia designed the interiors in gray and white, giving the gallery a calm, peaceful quality. The Museum of Modern Art (MoMA) was just down the block, and Stieglitz considered it a competitor. Despite his objections, Georgia loaned several of her paintings to MoMA for a group show.

In February 1930, her solo exhibit opened. Many of the paintings were from New Mexico. Critics raved about her work. A reviewer for the *New York Times* wrote, "What you will find at An American Place is the most exciting O'Keeffe show this writer has ever seen."

Several well-known museums bought paintings from the show, as did the mysterious collector who had bought Georgia's calla lilies for a huge sum. As Georgia grew more and more successful, she said simply, "I am a lucky person."

In April she went to Maine for a week and painted every day. When she came home, she received an invitation from Mabel to come to Taos for another summer. Again, Georgia agonized about going. Separations from Stieglitz were painful for both of them. She wanted his approval, and he gave the trip his blessing.

Before departing, she went to Lake George in early May to prepare the house for him and plant the garden. In the woods, she found a patch of early blooming jack-in-the-pulpits. "Remembering the art lessons of my high school days," she said, "I looked at the Jacks with great interest. I did a set of six paintings of them."

When Georgia had completed the work, she left for the Southwest. She said, "I must go for the summer months if I am to continue to live and to paint."

Jack-in-Pulpit-No. 2, 1930.

Ram's Head, White Hollyhock—Hills, 1935.

During the summer of 1930, Georgia discovered the village of Alcalde in the Rio Grande Valley. "It was the shapes of the hills there that fascinated me," she said.

She rented a cottage on the H and M Ranch. Some days she walked for miles to sketch and paint. Other times Georgia painted right in the car. She would drive to a spot that interested her, unbolt and swivel the driver's seat, sit in the back, and prop her canvas on the front seat. When curious people came along and watched what she was doing, she'd immediately pack up and move on somewhere else.

Georgia struggled to find a way of portraying the vast grandeur of the desert. "I have wanted to paint the desert, but I haven't known how," she later wrote in an exhibition catalog. During long walks, she began collecting bleached animal skeletons. "I don't think of them as bones," she said. To her they were beautiful shapes. She picked up bones, cow skulls, and horse skulls and took them back to the cottage. These were her "treasures," she told her friend Anita. "To me they are strangely more living than the animals walking around."

By the end of August, she had accumulated a big collection of skulls. Georgia carefully packed them in a wooden barrel, which she stuffed with fabric roses from fiestas to keep the skulls from breaking.

When the barrel arrived at Lake George, Stieglitz was horrified at the expense. Sixteen dollars (the equivalent of two hundred dollars today) for shipping a bunch of old bones! But later that year he photographed Georgia's fingers delicately exploring the teeth of a horse's skull and arranging a white bone on a piece of black cloth for a still life.

The following summer, in 1931, Georgia again traveled to New Mexico. When she came back to Lake George in July she began a new series of paintings. At some point she had placed a horse's skull on a table in the dining room, and one morning, while she was upstairs sorting her cloth flowers, Georgia heard someone at the front door. She walked downstairs with a pink rose in her hand but thought she would look silly holding it. "Almost without thinking about what I was doing," she said, "I put the flower in the horse's eye and went to the door. On my return, I was so struck by the wonderful effect of the rose in the horse's eye that I knew that here was a painting that had to be done."

She said that as she was working, she thought of the men in New York who so often talked of writing the Great American Novel or the Great American Play. "The people who talk about the American scene don't know anything about it," she said, whereas she knew and loved the United States, having driven cross-country many times. "As I painted along on my cow's skull on blue, I thought to myself, 'I'll make it an American painting,'" she wrote. "It gave me pleasure to make it in red, white, and blue."

To her surprise, Stieglitz liked the new "weird" paintings and exhibited them just before Christmas. Critics were astounded. "These original works . . . are Miss O'Keeffe's best," wrote McBride. Others interpreted Georgia's paintings as expressions of a morbid fascination with death. Georgia insisted that the idea behind the bones and flowers was to portray *life* on the desert.

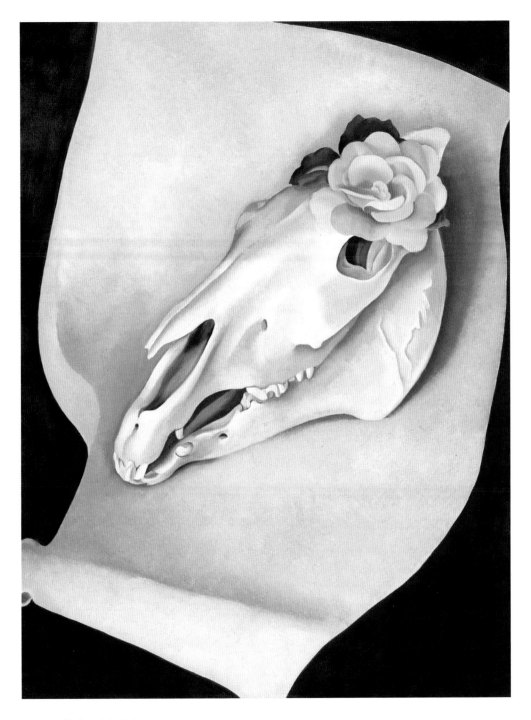

Horse's Skull with Pink Rose, 1931.

Gerald's Tree I, 1937.

But perhaps others saw dark feelings of loss that were really there. Even though Georgia was happy with her reviews, she was troubled by things in her life. Her husband was developing a close relationship with a young married woman who assisted him at the gallery. Rumors spread that they were having a love affair, and Georgia suspected this was true. Despite her anger and distress, Georgia didn't want to end her marriage. At the last minute she decided to stay at Lake George that summer instead of going to New Mexico.

At the lake, Georgia worked on an assignment that she had accepted earlier in the summer. She had been commissioned to paint a mural for the ladies' powder room at the new Radio City Music Hall in Rockefeller Center. Stieglitz violently opposed the project. He felt that she had lowered her standards by agreeing to do a painting for a small fee. They fought it out. In late November, six weeks before the Music Hall was to open, she went to the city to start painting. Her canvas had been hung on the curved walls of the powder room. But the workmen were behind schedule and had hurried. The plaster was not yet dry and ready for the canvas. As Georgia looked around the room she saw a piece of the canvas coming loose. After lunch another section loosened up. She announced that she wouldn't do the mural and walked off the job. Stieglitz was pleased that Georgia wasn't going to do the mural after all. But she considered this experience a public failure.

Georgia had lost confidence in herself as an artist and as a wife and became deeply depressed. She was forty-five years old. She couldn't eat, sleep, or even go for a walk. She suffered painful headaches and weeping spells. No one knew what was wrong or how to help her. On February 1, 1933, she was admitted to Doctors Hospital for psychiatric care and bed rest. It was uncertain whether Georgia would ever paint again.

Purple Hills, Ghost Ranch – 2/Purple Hills No II, 1934.

Ghost Ranch 15

Slowly Georgia began to get well. She was released from the hospital in the spring and went to Lake George for the summer. Georgia spent most of her time resting. She had adopted a stray white cat and named her Long Tail. Georgia loved to sit with Long Tail in her lap, the cat purring contentedly.

For more than a year Georgia did no artwork. Little by little, though, she regained her strength and felt more like her old self. In January 1934 she wrote to a friend, "I seem to have come out of my daze into another world—feeling very good—as though there is nothing the matter with me any more." And once again she began painting.

By June she was ready to return to New Mexico. She remembered Ghost Ranch and the desert landscape she had glimpsed one summer. She was intrigued by stories she had heard about the ranch. Supposedly it was haunted by evil spirits. The name was a rough translation of the Spanish *Rancho de los Brujos*, Ranch of Witches. According to legend, a family had been murdered there, and from time to time a ghostly woman carrying a baby appeared in the house. Georgia *had* to find the ranch.

One day while she was in the town of Española to buy groceries, she spotted a car with the initials "GR" on the side. When the driver, a cowboy, came out of the store, she asked him if he came from Ghost Ranch. He did, and he gave her directions for getting there. Georgia set out the next day.

She followed a dirt road up along the twisting Chama River, then made a right at the turn marked by a skull propped against a rock. On the plateau she found a cluster of bungalows owned by a wealthy Easterner. "I knew the minute I got up here that this was where I would live," she later told a reporter.

Georgia asked for a room. The owner said one would be available the next day. There was no telephone or electricity, just kerosene lamps for light. A perfect setup for Georgia.

She loved the harsh dry land, the wind, the stillness, the red hills, pink cliffs, and distant mountains. Every day she hiked for miles exploring the area. When a Ghost Ranch wrangler spotted her striding across the grassy plain, he reined in his horse and greeted her. She asked if he had seen any animal skulls. When he said yes and offered to get them for her, she said she preferred collecting them herself and asked where to find them.

Once, Georgia made a drawing of an ox skull and gave it as a gift to the ranch owner, Arthur Pack, who had become her friend. Pack immediately adopted the drawing as the logo of the Ghost Ranch, and it still is to this day.

Georgia rose at six in the morning and stayed out painting till six-thirty in the evening. Because of the intense heat, she traded her usual black attire for white cotton clothes that she made herself and wore sneakers or canvas shoes with rope soles. When guests at the ranch saw her they said, "Why don't you come in out of the heat?" Georgia smiled, shook her head, and continued to paint.

After dinner she often walked out to a high mesa to enjoy the sunset. Although she yearned to sleep outdoors, she admitted that she was "terribly afraid of snakes." To McBride she wrote, "It galls me that I haven't the courage to sleep out there in the hills alone—but I haven't."

In the fall she joined Stieglitz at Lake George. Despite their past tensions and conflicts, they still loved each other. Georgia felt more confident about taking charge of her life and doing what was best for her as an artist.

So the following year, she stayed at Ghost Ranch for six months from June through November. It was a particularly productive period. She painted pictures of turkey feathers, kachina dolls, sunflowers, blue morning glories, lavender hills, and bones.

The painting *Ram's Head, White Hollyhock—Hills* introduces a surreal, dreamlike theme. A large skull and flower float above hills dotted with clumps of sage. Of this painting Georgia said, "I don't remember where I picked up the head—or the hollyhock... My paintings sometimes grow by pieces from what is around."

When the painting was exhibited in her next annual show in New York, Lewis Mumford, art critic for the *New Yorker* raved, "In conception and execution, this is one of the most brilliant paintings O'Keeffe has done."

That year Georgia received a commission for a flower painting from Elizabeth Arden Beauty Salon. Georgia was delighted. The project fulfilled her "desire to paint something for a particular place—and paint it Big." The canvas was six feet tall and seven and a half feet wide, the largest work she had ever done. The subject was four enormous jimsonweeds, a poisonous flower that grows in the Southwest. To do the painting, Georgia needed a bigger studio. So she and Stieglitz moved from the Shelton to a penthouse apartment on East Fifty-fourth Street, overlooking the East River. And she hired a cook-housekeeper. From then on, Georgia always had someone in the city or at Lake George to take care of Stieglitz while she was gone.

Stieglitz was pleased with the project, too, because Arden agreed to pay the sum of ten thousand dollars. For Georgia, the success of the painting made up for the failure she had experienced at Radio City Music Hall.

And as what she thought was a treat, Arden, the owner of the salon, insisted on giving Georgia a makeover to show her what cosmetics could do. Afterward, Georgia took one look at herself and rushed home to wash off the makeup.

In the summer of 1937, Georgia drove to Ghost Ranch without letting Arthur Pack know her plans. When she arrived, he told her that all the cottages were full. She suggested that he kick someone out to make room for her. He thought for a moment, then took her to see Rancho de los Burros, the house he had built for his first wife. Pack unlocked the door of the small, U-shaped adobe house. Inside, the whitewashed rooms surrounded a patio, and the bedroom window looked out at the dramatic cliffs.

"As soon as I saw it, I knew I must have it," said Georgia. She stayed there all summer and did many paintings of the house and its view.

The patio faced a flat-topped mesa called Cerro Pedernal, about ten miles away. When visitors came over, Georgia took them outside and said, "Look at my front yard!" She called the Pedernal "a perfect blue mountain," and painted different versions of it: one in soft blues, another with red hills in the foreground and white clouds above, and still another with a gigantic pink hollyhock alongside.

"It's my private mountain," she joked. "It belongs to me. God told me if I painted it enough, I could have it."

The house (and view) officially became hers in October 1940 when she bought it from the Packs. Georgia let sagebrush and jimsonweed grow wild in the patio. She covered the low jimsonweed with chicken wire to keep her kitten from nibbling the poisonous flowers. To a friend she wrote, "Colored earth—rattlesnakes and a Siamese kitten for news is all I have . . . This is the magical country for me."

Jimson Weed, White Flower No. 1, 1932.

Untitled (Abstraction), 1943

With my own eye 16

Each year it became harder for Georgia to tear herself away from Ghost Ranch. At night she often climbed a handmade ladder to the flat roof of the adobe and watched the stars.

On long walks, Georgia discovered different objects that gave her ideas for paintings. Animal pelvis bones, for instance. "I do not remember picking up the first one," she wrote, "but I remember from when I first noticed them always knowing I would one day be painting them. . . . I held one up against the sky and saw the blue through that hole. They were most wonderful against the Blue. . . . When I started painting the pelvis bones, I was most interested in the holes in the bones—what I saw through them."

Stieglitz understood. Georgia returned to him every winter out of affection and a sense of loyalty and obligation. When she went back to New York, she left her Siamese cats, Annie and Anselmo, with a friend and hired someone to take care of her house. In October 1940, she met Maria Chabot, a young woman from Texas who was an aspiring writer. Maria admired Georgia and her paintings, and Georgia enjoyed Maria's lively company. Maria agreed to run the house in exchange for room and board, and the arrangement gave Georgia more time for painting when she was at Ghost Ranch.

Georgia and Maria tried to raise vegetables at Ghost Ranch, but the soil was too dry and sandy. In 1941 the United States entered World War II.

Maria rented a parcel of land in the nearby village of Abiquiu for a Victory Garden to help the war effort. Like millions of Americans, she raised some of their own food so that more supplies could be shipped to the troops. Georgia wrote to her sister Claudie, "When there is no meat we eat beans."

During the war years it was especially difficult to live at Ghost Ranch without a phone or electricity or enough fuel to drive the forty miles to Española for supplies. Georgia began to think of acquiring a second house where she could grow more of her own food and be closer to town when there was bad weather. Before settling at Ghost Ranch she had looked around Abiquiu and had seen a ruined hacienda. She had climbed over the crumbling wall and walked around. In the large patio there was a long wall with a door on one side. The door caught her attention. "The wall with a door in it was something I had to have," she said.

She tried to buy the house, but the man who owned it wanted six thousand dollars. "Too much," said Georgia. A few years later the man died and left the property to the Catholic Church. In 1945 when Georgia went back to see it, the buildings were toppling down, the roofs had caved in, and pigs and cattle wandered around the place. However, the patio wall with the door was standing. Georgia, still captivated by that door, pressed the Church into selling it to her. "I had no peace until I bought the house."

She started a series of paintings titled *In the Patio* by doing pencil sketches, then oils. "I'm always trying to paint that door," she said. "I never quite get it. It's a curse—the way I feel about that door."

The house needed work to make it livable, and Georgia began renovations. She asked Maria to take charge of the project. Adobe bricks were handmade from the earth on Georgia's land, the roof was restored, and plumbing and electricity installed.

Georgia O'Keeffe's Abiquiu house, patio, undated, photograph by Georgia O'Keeffe.

Meanwhile, Georgia corresponded with James Johnson Sweeney, curator at MoMA, for an exhibition showing examples of her entire life's work, ranging from the early paintings and drawings to recent pieces. Georgia, age fifty-eight, was the first woman artist ever chosen to have a major show at the distinguished museum.

Sweeney asked her to send critics' past reviews for the catalog. Georgia told him to not take the enthusiastic reviews too seriously. "I always thought it didn't matter much," she wrote.

But she did say, "I think that what I have done is something rather unique in my time and that I am one of the few who gives our country a voice of its own . . . I claim no credit—it is only that I have seen with my own eye."

Georgia flew to New York for the opening. At the reception on May 15, 1946, in a plain black silk dress, she was the only woman not attired in an evening gown. Fifty-seven of her paintings, some drawings, and a watercolor were displayed in four galleries. The rooms were so crowded that people had to come back to actually see the art. A visitor gushed with excitement over Georgia's work and said he couldn't find words to express his feelings.

"Oh, no," she said to him, "it's just ordinary. I think each painting is fine after I've done it. But that wears off. It's just part of my daily life."

Yet in a letter to Maria who was in Abiquiu, Georgia revealed her pride. "I believe that my show is what you call a success," she wrote.

Stieglitz was genuinely pleased too. He wrote, "Incredible, Georgia—and how beautiful your pictures are at the [Museum of Modern Art]—I'm glad."

Years later when a journalist remarked about her painting and the risks she had taken, Georgia said, "I've never thought of myself as having a great gift. . . It isn't just talent. You have to have something else. You have to have a kind of nerve. It's mostly a lot of nerve, and a lot of very, very hard work."

In The Patio, VIII, 1950.

Georgia O'Keeffe in Abiquiu Studio, 1976, photograph by Fred Mang, Jr., Courtesy of The National Park Service.

Still painting 17

After the opening of the show at MoMA, Georgia returned to Abiquiu. In July she received a telegram that Stieglitz was seriously ill; she flew back to New York to be at his bedside. On July 13, 1946, at the age of eighty-two, Stieglitz died. Georgia buried his ashes at Lake George. She wrote, "I put him where he could hear the Lake." Georgia inherited his entire estate and spent the next two years cataloging and distributing 850 works of modern art and hundreds of photographs.

Finally, by 1948, she had time to resume painting. In 1949 her house in Abiquiu was finished, and she moved to New Mexico permanently, spending summers at Ghost Ranch and winters in Abiquiu. For the next twenty-two years, Georgia kept working. At age seventy-five, she told an inquiring journalist, "Why of course I'm still painting! I'm not old or worn out."

In 1970 *Life* magazine featured her in a cover story celebrating not only her art, but her unique Western lifestyle. Famous photographers came to Abiquiu to take pictures of her sitting among her collection of stones and skulls and in her studio. Some photos show her walking along the hills with her Chows.

Nearly two decades earlier she was given a Chow puppy as a gift. From then on, she always kept Chows, which she called her "little people." The dogs accompanied her on early morning and evening hikes and slept in her bedroom at night.

With all the publicity, a new generation of admirers dropped by hoping to meet her. Once, when a stranger came to the door and asked Georgia what she was painting, she snapped, "Nothing—because I'm talking to you!"

While young female artists often regarded her as a role model, she thought of herself simply as a painter. Yet in 1971 upon accepting an honor at Bryn Mawr, a women's college, she spoke encouragingly to the art students. "Paint what's in your head, what you are acquainted with," she said. "Even if you think it doesn't count—and for some of you it may not—doing something that is entirely your own may be pretty exciting."

In 1971, at age eighty-four, Georgia's eyesight began to fail. No longer able to paint, she began working in clay with the guidance of a young potter, Juan Hamilton. He had shown up one day looking for a job and became her assistant, representative, and close friend.

By 1984 Georgia had become too frail to stay in Abiquiu and moved to a house in Santa Fe, where she could be near medical care. On March 6, 1986, a few minutes after noon, she died. She was ninety-eight. News reached Abiquiu just before dusk, and a villager began to ring the bells of the little adobe church.

Georgia had once said, "When I think of death, I only regret that I will not be able to see this beautiful country any more, unless the Indians are right and my spirit will walk here after I'm gone."

The Indians *were* right. Anyone visiting Abiquiu and Ghost Ranch knows that Georgia's wild and wonderful spirit lives on.

Mesa and Road East, 1952.

Bibliography

Materials marked with an asterisk (*) are suitable for younger readers.

Books

Bardwell, John D. *Old York Beach* and *Old York Beach, Volume II*. Charleston, S.C.: Arcadia Books, 1994 and 1996.

* Benke, Britta. *Georgia O'Keeffe: The Artist in the Desert*. Munich: Prestel Verlag, 2006.

Danly, Susan. *Georgia O'Keeffe and the Camera: The Art of Identity*. New Haven: Yale University Press in Association with The Portland Museum of Art, Maine, 2008.

Drohojowska-Philp, Hunter. *Full Bloom: The Art and Life of Georgia O'Keeffe*. New York: W.W. Norton & Company, 2004.

Giboire, Clive, editor. *Lovingly, Georgia: The Complete Correspondence of Georgia O'Keeffe & Anita Pollitzer*. New York: A Touchstone Book published by Simon & Schuster Inc., 1990.

Haskell, Barbara. *Georgia O'Keeffe: Works on Paper*. Santa Fe: Museum of New Mexico Press, 1985.

Lisle, Laurie. *Portrait of an Artist: A Biography of Georgia O'Keeffe*. New York: Washington Square Press, 1986.

Lynes, Barbara Buhler. *Georgia O'Keeffe: Catalog Raisonne*, Volumes One and Two. New Haven: Yale University Press in Association with National Gallery of Art, Washington, and The Georgia O'Keeffe Foundation, Abiquiu, New Mexico, 1999.

Lynes, Barbara Buhler, Lesley Poling-Kempes, and Frederick W. Turner. *Georgia O'Keeffe and New Mexico: A Sense of Place*. Princeton and Oxford: Princeton University Press, 2004.

Lynes, Barbara Buhler, and Ann Paden, editors. *Maria Chabot–Georgia O'Keeffe: Correspondence, 1941-1949*. Santa Fe: Georgia O'Keeffe Museum Research Center, 2003.

Naef, Weston, general editor. In Focus: Alfred Stieglitz. Malibu, California: The J. Paul Getty Museum, 1995.

* O'Keeffe, Georgia. *Some Memories of Drawings*, edited by Doris Bry. Albuquerque: University of New Mexico Press, 1974.

* _____*Georgia O'Keeffe*. New York: Viking Press, A Studio Book, 1976.

Peters, Sarah Whitaker. *Becoming O'Keeffe: The Early Years*. New York: The Abbeville Press, 2001.

Pollitzer, Anita. *A Woman on Paper: Georgia O'Keeffe*. New York: A Touchstone Book, Published by Simon & Schuster Inc., 1988.

Robinson, Roxana. *Georgia O'Keeffe: A Life*. Hanover and London: University Press of New England, 1989.

Shattuck, Roger, Thomas West, Nicholas Callaway, Belinda Rathbone, and Elisabeth H. Turner. *Two Lives: Georgia O'Keeffe and Alfred Stieglitz: A Conversation in Paintings and Photographs.* New York: Callaway Editions in association with The Phillips Collection, 1992.

* Venezia, Mike. *Georgia O'Keeffe.* Danbury, Connecticut: Children's Press, 1993.
* Winter, Jeanette. *My Name Is Georgia.* New York: Harcourt Inc., Voyager Books 1998.

ARTICLES
Calvin Tomkins, "The Rose in the Eye Looked Pretty Fine." *The New Yorker,* March 4, 1974.
Calvin Tomkins, "Look to the Things Around You." *The New Yorker,* September 16, 1974.

VIDEOS
Georgia O'Keeffe: A Life in Art. Produced, directed, and written by Perry Miller Adato, executive producer, Barbara Buhler Lynes. Santa Fe: Georgia O'Keeffe Museum, 2002.

Image Credits

Cover Georgia O'Keeffe, *Red Hills with the Pedernal (Pedernal with Red Hills)*, 1936, oil on linen, 19 3/4 x 29 3/4 in (50.16 x 75.56 cm). Collection of the New Mexico Museum of Art. Bequest of Helen Miller Jones, 1986 (1986.137.18).

Chabot, Maria. *Georgia O'Keeffe Hitching a Ride to Abiquiu, Ghost Ranch*, 1944. Georgia O'Keeffe Musem (1998.04.01) © Georgia O'Keefe Museum.

Page 8 Georgia O'Keeffe Museum Research Center Library, O'Keeffe Painting Materials, Display Drawer, Santa Fe, New Mexico. Gift of Juan and Anna Marie Hamilton, 1998. © Georgia O'Keeffe Museum. Photography by Malcolm Varon.

Page 10 Georgia O'Keeffe, 1903. Georgia O'Keeffe Museum, Georgia O'Keeffe Foundation Photograph Collection. Gift of the Georgia O'Keeffe Foundation, 2006 (2006-06-0706). © Georgia O'Keeffe Museum.

Page 13 *Untitled (Catherine O'Keeffe)*, 1904. Georgia O'Keeffe. Graphite on paper, 12 x 9 in (30.48 x 22.86 cm). Georgia O'Keeffe Museum. Gift of The Georgia O'Keeffe Foundation (2006.05.009). © 2010 Georgia O'Keeffe Museum / Artists Rights Society (ARS), New York.

Page 14 *Untitled (Hand)*, 1902. Georgia O'Keeffe. Graphite on paper, 6 x 9 in (16.51 x 23.49 cm). Gift of The Georgia O'Keeffe Foundation (2006.05.002). © 2010 Georgia O'Keeffe Museum / Artists Rights Society (ARS), New York.

Page 17 *Untitled (Vase of Flowers)*, 1903 / 1905. Georgia O'Keeffe. Graphite on paper, 17 3/4 x 11 1/2 in (45.08 x 29.21). Georgia O'Keeffe Museum. Gift of The Georgia O'Keeffe Foundation (2006.05.003). © 2010 The Georgia O'Keeffe Museum / Artists Rights Society (ARS), New York.

Page 19 The Class of 1905, Chatham Hall. Courtesy of Chatham Hall.

Page 20 *Untitled (Teapot and Flowers)*, 1903/1905. Georgia O'Keeffe. Graphite on paper, 12 1/4 x 16 3/4 in (31.11 x 42.54 cm). Georgia O'Keeffe Museum. Gift of The Georgia O'Keeffe Foundation (2006.05.004). © 2010 Georgia O'Keeffe Museum / Artists Rights Society (ARS), New York.

Page 23 Georgia O'Keeffe and Family, c. 1916. Georgia O'Keeffe Museum, Georgia O'Keeffe Foundation Photograph Collection. Gift of the Georgia O'Keeffe Foundation, 2006 (2006-06-0710). © Georgia O'Keeffe Museum.

Page 24 Eugene Speicher, *Portrait of Georgia O'Keeffe*, 1908, oil on canvas, 21 x 18 in Permanent Collection, The Art Students League of New York.

Page 26–27 William Merritt Chase Conducting a Class at the Art Students League, New York, 1907. Courtesy of The Art Students League.

Page 30 *Untitled (Rotunda - University of Virginia)*, 1912–1914. Graphite on paper, 11 7/8 x 9 (30.16 x 22.86 cm). Georgia O'Keeffe Museum. Gift of The Georgia O'Keeffe Foundation (2006.05.608) © 2010 Georgia O'Keeffe Museum / Artists Rights Society (ARS), New York.

Page 35 Clark, John Spencer. Library of Congress. A page from the teacher's manual for Prang's shorter course in form study and drawing. Boston, New York [etc.] The Prang Educational Company: 1888. http://lccn.loc.gov/09021447 (accessed September 24, 2010).

Page 36 Library of Congress. Cover of *291*, No. 4. New York, Arno Press: 1915. http://lccn.loc.gov/00204566 (accessed September 24, 2010).

Page 40 *No. 17 - Special*, 1919. Georgia O'Keeffe. Charcoal on paper, 19 3/4 x 12 3/4 in (50.2 x 32.4 cm). Georgia O'Keeffe Museum. Gift of The Burnett Foundation and The Georgia O'Keeffe Foundation (1997.05.16). © 2010 Georgia O'Keeffe Museum / Artists Rights Society (ARS), New York.

Page 43 Georgia O'Keeffe in Canyon, Texas, 1916 or 1917. Georgia O'Keeffe Museum, Georgia O'Keeffe Foundation Photograph Collection. Gift of the Georgia O'Keeffe Foundation, 2006 (2006-06-0747). © Georgia O'Keeffe Museum.

Page 44 Käsebier, Gertrude. Library of Congress. Alfred Stieglitz. 1902. http://www.loc.gov/pictures/item/2006691707/ (accessed September 24, 2010).

Page 49 *No 22 – Special*, 1916–1917. Georgia O'Keeffe. Oil on board, 13 1/8 x 17 in (33.3 x 43.8 cm). Georgia O'Keeffe Museum. Gift of The Burnett Foundation and The Georgia O'Keeffe Foundation (1997.05.16). © 2010 The Georgia O'Keeffe Museum / Artists Rights Society (ARS), New York.

Page 51 Stieglitz, Alfred. Georgia O'Keeffe, 1918. http://commons.wikimedia.org/wiki/File:O%27Keeffe-(hands).jpg (accessed September 24, 2010).

Page 52 *Evening Star VI*, 1917. Georgia O'Keeffe. Watercolor on paper, 8 7/8 x 12 in (22.5 x 30.5 cm). Georgia O'Keeffe Museum. Gift of The Burnett Foundation and The Georgia O'Keeffe Foundation (1997.18.03). © 2010 The Georgia O'Keeffe Museum / Artists Rights Society (ARS), New York.

Page 56 Stieglitz, Alfred. Library of Congress. Georgia O'Keeffe, 1919. Library of Congress, Prints & Photographs Division, The Alfred Stieglitz Collection, Gift of The Georgia O'Keeffe Foundation and Library Purchase, [reproduction number, e.g., LC-USZ62-123456]. http://www.loc.gov/pictures/item/2005679119/ (accessed September 24, 2010).

Page 59 Georgia O'Keeffe 1887-1986, *Music - Pink and Blue II*, 1919. Oil on canvas, Overall: 35 x 29⅛ in (88.9 x 74 cm). Whitney Museum of American Art, New York; Gift of Emily Fisher Landau in honor of Tom Armstrong 91.90. © The Georgia O'Keeffe Foundation/Artists Rights Society (ARS), New York. Photograph by Sheldan C. Collins.

Page 61 Georgia O'Keeffe 1920/1922. Alfred Stieglitz. Palladium print, 4½ x 3⁹⁄₁₆ in (11.43 x 9.05 cm). Georgia O'Keeffe Museum. Gift of The Georgia O'Keeffe Museum. © Artists Rights Society (ARS), New York. Photo credit: Georgia O'Keeffe Museum, Santa Fe / Art Resource, New York.

Page 62 *House and Trees, Lake George*, 1932. Alfred Stieglitz. Gelatin silver print, 7⁵⁄₁₆ x 9⁵⁄₁₆ in (18.57 x 23.65 cm). Georgia O'Keeffe Museum. Gift of The Georgia O'Keeffe Foundation (2003.01.22). © 2010 Georgia O'Keeffe Museum / Artists Rights Society (ARS), New York.

Page 65 *Apple Family—2*, 1920. Georgia O'Keeffe. Oil on canvas. 8⅛ x 10⅛ in (20.6 x 25.7 cm). Georgia O'Keeffe Museum. Gift of The Burnett Foundation and The Georgia O'Keeffe Foundation (1997.04.03). © 2010 The Georgia O'Keeffe Museum / Artists Rights Society (ARS), New York.

Page 66 *Two Pink Shells/Pink Shell*, 1937. Georgia O'Keeffe. Oil on canvas, 12 x 10 in (30.5 x 25.4 cm). Gift of The Burnett Foundation and The Georgia O'Keeffe Foundation (1997.04.05). © 2010 The Georgia O'Keeffe Museum / Artists Rights Society (ARS), New York.

Page 68 *Calla Lily Turned Away*, 1923. Georgia O'Keeffe. Pastel on paper-based cardboard, 14 x 10⅞ in (52.1 x 41.9 cm). Gift of The Burnett Foundation (1997.18.02). © 2010 The Georgia O'Keeffe Museum / Artists Rights Society (ARS), New York.

Page 71 *Calla Lily in Tall Glass—No. 2*, 1923. Georgia O'Keeffe. Oil on board. 32⅛ x 12 in (81.6 x 30.5 cm). Georgia O'Keeffe Museum. Gift of The Burnett Foundation (1997.06.10). © 2010 Georgia O'Keeffe Museum / Artists Rights Society (ARS), New York.

Page 73 Georgia O'Keeffe and Alfred Stieglitz at Lake George New York, 1929. Alfred Stieglitz/ Georgia O'Keeffe Archive. Yale Collection of American Literature, Beinecke Rare Book and Manuscript Library, Yale University.

Page 74 Georgia O'Keeffe American, 1887-1986, *The Shelton with Sunspots, NY*, 1926. Oil on canvas, 48½ x 30¼ in. (123.2 x 76.8 cm), Gift of Leigh B. Block, 1985.206, The Art Institute of Chicago. Photography © The Art Institute of Chicago.

Page 77 Georgia O'Keeffe, *Radiator Building - Night, New York*, 1927, Oil on canvas, Gift of Georgia O'Keeffe, Fisk University Galleries.

Page 80 *Corn No. 2*, 1924. Georgia O'Keeffe. Oil on canvas, 27¼ x 10 in (69.2 x 25.4 cm). Georgia O'Keeffe Museum. Gift of The Burnett Foundation and The Georgia O'Keeffe Foundation (1997.04.06). © 2010 Georgia O'Keeffe Museum / Artists Rights Society (ARS), New York.

Page 83 *Georgia O'Keeffe—After Return from New Mexico*, 1929. Alfred Stieglitz. Gelatin silver print. 3¹⁄₁₆ x 4⅝ in (7.78 x 11.75 cm). Georgia O'Keeffe Museum. Gift of The Georgia O'Keeffe

Foundation (2003.01.15). © 2010 Georgia O'Keeffe Museum / Artists Rights Society (ARS), New York.

Page 85 *D.H. Lawrence Pine Tree*, 1929. Georgia O'Keeffe. Oil on canvas, 31 x 40 in (78.75 x 101.6 cm). The Ella Gallup Sumner and Mary Catlin Sumner Collection (1981.23). © 2010 Georgia O'Keeffe Museum / Artist Rights Society (ARS), New York.

Page 87 *Jack-in-Pulpit – No. 2*, Alfred Stieglitz Collection, Bequest of Georgia O'Keeffe, Image courtesy National Gallery of Art, Washington, 1930, oil on canvas, 40 x 30 in (101.6 x 76.2 cm).

Page 88 *Ram's Head, White Hollyhock-Hills*, 1935, oil on canvas, 30 x 36 in (76.2 x 91.5 cm). Brooklyn Museum. 1992.11.28. Bequest of Edith and Milton Lowenthal.

Page 91 O'Keeffe, Georgia (1887–1986) © ARS, NY, *Horse's Skull with Pink Rose*, 1931. Oil on canvas, 40 x 30 in (101.6 x 76.2 cm). Gift of the Georgia O'Keeffe Foundation.

Page 92 *Gerald's Tree I*, 1937. Georgia O'Keeffe. Oil on canvas, 40 x 30⅛ in (101.6 x 76.5 cm). Georgia O'Keeffe Museum. Gift of The Burnett Foundation (1997.06.35). © 2010 The Georgia O'Keeffe Museum / Artists Rights Society (ARS), New York.

Page 94 *Purple Hills, Ghost Ranch— 2 / Purple Hills No. II*, 1934. Georgia O'Keeffe. Oil on canvas affixed to masonite, 16¼ x 30¼ in (41.3 x 76.8 cm). Georgia O'Keeffe Museum. Gift of The Burnett Foundation (1997.06.20). © 2010 Georgia O'Keeffe Museum / Artists Rights Society (ARS), New York.

Page 99 and Cover *Jimson Weed, White flower no. 1*, 1932. Georgia O'Keeffe. Oil on canvas, 48 x 40 in (121.9 x 101.6 cm). Gift of The Burnett Foundation. © 2010 Georgia O'Keeffe Museum / Artists Rights Society (ARS), New York.

Page 100 *Untitled (Abstraction)*, 1943. Georgia O'Keeffe. Charcoal and chalk on paper, 24 x 17⅞ in. Georgia O'Keeffe Museum. Gift of The Georgia O'Keeffe Foundation. © 2010 Georgia O'Keeffe Musem / Artist Rights Society (ARS), New York.

Page 103 *Georgia O'Keeffe's Abiquiu House, Patio*, undated. Georgia O'Keeffe. Georgia O'Keeffe Museum, Georgia O'Keeffe Foundation Photograph Collection. Gift of the Georgia O'Keeffe Foundation, 2006 (2006-06-1398). © Georgia O'Keeffe Museum.

Page 105 *In the Patio, VIII*, 1950. Georgia O'Keeffe. Oil on canvas, 26 x 20 in (66.04 x 50.8 cm). Georgia O'Keeffe Museum. Gift of The Burnett Foundation and The Georgia O'Keeffe Foundation (1997.05.08). © 2010 Georgia O'Keeffe Museum / Artists Rights Society (ARS), New York.

Page 106 *Georgia O'Keeffe in Abiquiu Studio*, 1976. Fred Mang, Jr. Georgia O'Keeffe Museum Archives. Photo credit: The National Park Service and Fred Mang, Jr.

Page 109 *Mesa and Road East*, 1952. Georgia O'Keeffe. Oil on canvas, 26 x 36 in (66.04 x 91.44 cm). Georgia O'Keeffe Museum. Gift of The Georgia O'Keeffe Foundation (2006.05.234). © 2010 Georgia O'Keeffe Museum / Artists Rights Society (ARS), New York.

Index